Best Wishes
to
Professor Lawrence
from
John & Satsuko Bleibler

SEMANTIC DIALOGUES

or

Ethics versus Rhetoric

John T. Blackmore

Setsuko Tanaka

This book is published by Sentinel Open Press and
distributed by Enfield Publishing & Distribution Co.
P.O. Box 699, Enfield NH. 234 May Street, 03748
Telephone 603-632-5611.

Printed by
Signature Book Printing,
www.sbpbooks.com

ISBN 978-0-578-05719-4 $25.00

52500>

9 780578 057194

TABLE OF CONTENTS

Recent Books jointly by
J. Blackmore, R. Itagaki & S. Tanaka

Ernst Mach's Vienna 1895-1930
Kluwer: Dordrecht, 2001. 345 pages

Ernst Mach's Science – Its Character
And Influence on Einstein and others
Tokai University Press, 2006, 304 pages

Ernst Mach's Philosophy – Pro and Con
2009, 253 pages, Enfield Publishing and
Distribution Co, 234 May Street, NH.

Ernst Mach's Influence Spreads, 2009,
485 pages, Enfield Publishing and Distribution Co., 234 May Street, Enfield NH.

Ernst Mach's Graz 1864-1867, 2010,
245 pages. Enfield Publishing and Distribution Co., 234 May Street, Enfield NH.

Ernst Mach's Prague 1867-1895, 2010
Forthcoming.

PREFACE

1

We are torn between a wish to be fair to all perspectives and an intent to support the point of view which we think is most reliable and needed at this point in history. Since it is hard to accomplish both ends, we have decided to employ dialogues which allow for different points of view and to indicate which one we think comes closest to being sound or correct.

Let us approach the issue of fairness first. It should be helpful to understand that fairness to one approach can mean unfairness to something else, and that one can always persuade oneself that something is unfair to someone. Ethics on the other hand is allegedly fixed since the ethical side of the Ten Commandments or something like it seems to be universally valid, that is, universal "Thou shallt nots" like stealing, lying, deception, and cheating, but because new editions of the Bible and perhaps other key works in other religions sometimes change the wording of some prohibitions, then confusion can sometimes arise. For example, earlier Bibles normally maintained a Commandment "Thou shallt not murder." But many later editions have altered that to "You shall not kill". But the difference is a major one. The first allows killing by soldiers and policemen if necessary to protect a society, while the second does not, indeed, logically makes them criminals if they do, and takes away their honor in being willing to die to protect others, thus weakening their resolve to defend us and civilization. Also, the ethics of avoiding sin and forgiving it are different. One leans to free will and the other not. These disagreements are important even in our restricted discussion of semantics, and are another reason for trying to be fair to other perspectives. Nevertheless, while we have our own point of view, we will still do our best to raise the strongest objections we can against our own position, and of course the strongest replies to them. We apologize if either one or both do not seem strong enough.

If one identifies causes with scientific laws, then one normally thinks that words, propositions, or both mean or have meaning and even that language and meaning may be objective, and that if this is an idealized perspective, then so be it. This is also a position widely supported by both dictionaries and habit since it is normal to take for granted that words mean or have meaning. In fact, it may even come as a surprise to some readers to discover that there are other views.

Our own position, however, is one of those other views, and it naturally follows from identifying causes not with laws but with influence, the capacity of one person or thing to at least partly influence other people or things, including language, meaning, and ideas, even if only a totality of all relevant factors may fully influence the behavior of anything. Indeed, while not as prominent or openly recognized as the dictionary view that words mean, we also commonly think of human beings choosing which language or words to employ and also which meaning or meanings to associate with words and language.

Our practice is not unusual or uncommon, but as a position it tends to be under-recognized. Instead of saying "words mean" we say or more often should say "people mean", since in the practical world it is particular persons at particular places and times who associate meaning with words which we call connotation. The root or most common descriptive association is usually called the denotation while emotional or value connotations are unfortunately rarely included in dictionaries. This is especially regrettable because in the so-called "real world" or at least the less-idealized or non-idealized world, connotations, especially value-connotations, are often more important than denotations or other descriptive connotations. On the other hand, words with strong value connotations can be found in *Roget's Thesaurus* and updated versions of it.

What are value-connotations? They are good and bad associations which color words and can prejudge whether what is being referred to is true or false. Partly because most dictionaries largely ignore them, like they ignore the perspective that meaning is primarily a matter of human intent and assumption, they are often overlooked when we actually speak or write. But consciously overlooked does not mean ineffective or without influence. In fact, since most assertion is not accompanied by evidence, it is the value-connotation of words which normally help persuade most people most of the time. In the absence of accompanying evidence persuasion by value-connotation can also be called a form of rhetoric, which raises the question of whether it is legitimate, that is, ethical, especially if the purpose of the user of words which have value-connotations is to persuade, and he or she realizes that in the absence of evidence that this can be or is wrong.

To this point, both believers that words or propositions mean and supporters of the position that actually particular persons mean can both agree that attempts at persuasion based on value-connotation and in the absence of accompanying evidence are improper. Why? Because they are deceptive; they help persuade on weak or insufficient grounds, that is, beyond what the weight of evidence justifies.

The rest of this introduction is for those readers who accept or lean toward or are at least willing to consider the "people mean" perspective as the more effective and helpful one in resisting rhetoric and replacing it with sound argument and reference to or direct presentation of weight of evidence:

This book even though it consists of dialogues in which we try to acknowledge and be fair to other perspectives is at least equally a defence of ethics against the growing use of rhetoric in advertising, politics, science, and philosophy. We oppose persuasion by illegitimate means, that is, without backing from the weight of evidence. We oppose failure to notice how the value-connotation of words, both good and bad, help rhetoric seduce readers and listeners. We oppose books designed to help people become more influential by socially ingratiating themselves rather than by developing moral character and becoming better educated. We oppose the notion that the latest idealized theories in semantics and philosophy represent the deepest understanding of semantics and philosophy.

We also oppose attempts to treat meaning and language as objective on the basis of dictionary meaning, convention, and the mere habit of expression and that words and propositions have fixed meanings when in fact the particular persons who actually use meaning and language are the main causal agents in determining what those persons are driving at, especially in conversation and communication where most words have value connotations and the double-meanings of satire, irony, humor, facetiousness, metaphor, and analogy. Such are typically of major importance and not just in spoken language, but in much human thinking and writing as well, as should be obvious for those of us who rely much more often on the rich content of improved versions of *Roget's thesaurus* than on the limited, restrictive, and much more dogmatic character of most dictionaries which largely ignore double-meaning and value-connotation, even if the words linked to them are mentioned.

Furthermore, we think that the value connotations of words refute the notion that most language and meaning are objective in the sense of being independent of human meaning as intent and underlying assumptions. We say this even though in our preference for honesty and ethical discourse we strongly favor being as fair and objective as possible. But this goal is not accomplished by pretending that what is largely subjective is objective, when it is not. To help further a solution we define two types of "objectivity" absolute objectivity as freedom from the possibility of being influenced by subjective factors like feeling and prejudice and relative objectivity as attempting to be as fair, honorable, just, and moral not only in expressing our ideas in language but in supporting and believing in rational and responsible ideas as well in the way we think and understand. Our goal is to help make what is generally considered to be the mental world as fair and objective as possible without self-deception about what is absolutely objective.

Our preference for a dialogue approach follows naturally from a wish to write as closely to what basic language as spoken language allows. There is not only a rich tradition in philosophy for doing this starting with Plato and his attempt to recapture the spoken language of Socrates, at least in the early dialogues, but spoken dialogue and the closest written approximations to it also allow for the importance of changes in tone of voice and verbal emphasis which can indicate what is actually meant much more clearly than mere expression in terms of dictionary meaning. Nor can the use of feeble written substitutes like italics, underlining, and quotation marks capture all of the deeper meanings intended and spoken, though they often help.

Since the objective style of writing in spite of its many advantages fails to capture all that is intended and assumed by writers, we think that the real solution where maximum communication is concerned is probably at least in a dialogue context to give personality and more emotional character to the participants, not because we prefer subjectivity to objectivity but because it is generally easier to catch the likely tone of voice and emphasis which speakers display, which can be so hard to actually include in most writing. It is the false notion of dictionary-based objectivity which seems to influence many writers especially in science and philosophy to *seem* objective at all cost in expression, regardless of how incomplete with respect to meaning and often emotional or prejudiced their actual thinking, understanding, and beliefs so often are.

We all admire expression which seems fair and neutral, without emotion or self-reference, but it can be hard to make people realize that the style which is most pleasing in science and in much everyday life can be disastrous where truth is concerned. Style is not content. The more agreeable the style or mode of communication, the more likely it is to persuade an audience in the absence of supporting weight of evidence. This may seem good for the speaker or writer, but not for science and truth. We are not opposed to an objective style. We prefer it ourselves, but because of its natural persuasive ability among educated people it is also the one most preferred in most successful scientific and scholarly persuasion, and hence is the most dangerous where truth is concerned, the approach where care and cautiousness are most required in order not to be seduced into believing what is false merely by style, especially when unaccompanied by strong evidence.

People often misunderstand rhetoric as if it were mostly fancy, literary, or emotional expression, and many people including ourselves are sometimes influenced favorably by that, but if rhetoric means persuasion without sufficient factual support, that is, from weight of evidence, then to repeat: the most seductive stylistic approach likely to persuade the most educated people is a straight objective style, even if the content is misleading or false, hence because these dialogues in this book are for people who are or want to become educated and understand what is most probably true, we have to warn as many people as we can about the dangers of an objective style, lest they be wrongly persuaded by what is basically irrelevant, namely style. Strictly speaking, truth means correspondence with non-idealized reality, and weight of evidence to that effect is the only fully legitimate type of persuasion.

Objectification of language and meaning, false as it is and false as the inference that objective style of writing is "most scientific", regardless of whether what is asserted is true or not, has been partly defended by no less a thinker than Sir Karl Popper who thinks all science is idealized and all its meaning objective, but no historian or supporter of non-idealized science can accept that, no friend of semantics as the study of real meaning can buy that, and of course no lover of truth and avoiding rhetoric can believe such claims without reservation either. Objective appearance like all appearance if mental may conceal a menagerie of prejudice and falsehood.

On the other side of the coin, disagreeable style which can vary from person to person is no evidence against truth. It may annoy us, but we must persevere in the search for truth in spite of such things. Many people dislike emotional presentation or too much reference to oneself, but truth is not determined by such things. Liars are not always liars and honest people are sometimes wrong. Only weight of evidence can decide, and evidence is a complex thing and can require considerable research plus good judgment.

Nor should we advocate or tolerate invidious distinctions which persuade by classifying other positions in a pejorative or unfair way such as between science and metaphysics as if the first were good and the second bad and as if they were incompatible with each other, when in fact reality (which is what metaphysics is primarily about) is a primary concern of most scientists even if they do not study or recognize that science itself rests on deeper assumptions about reality: semantic, epistemological, ontological, and value assumptions which may best be called foundation theory in order to avoid the bad-connotation which has long afflicted the word "metaphysics". The importance of philosophy as foundation theory rests on the natural assumption that nothing can be more important than the deepest presuppositions or premises underlying science and human understanding.

Fortunately, a major strength of using a dialogue method of presentation is that it readily allows for the expression of different points of view. Nor can we deceive ourselves into thinking that a majority of readers have fully accepted our own perspective yet. Hence, the reader will find much disagreement and controversy in these pages, largely because it is part of our conception of relative objectivity that we should try to be fair to all relevant points of view at least to the extent of allowing them to be heard and without distortion, even if we will naturally tend to favor our own point of view when we can fairly, honestly, and appropriately do so.

Rhetoric is a terrible thing, and teaching people to become more skilled at it, a so-called necessity with lawyers and even many teachers and politicians, is nothing to be proud of. What we can and should be proud of is a willingness to tell the truth when most people don't want to hear it, and hope that enough individuals have the strength of character to prefer evidence-supported argument to mere pleasing style. We need more people who love the search for truth and are willing to dedicate their lives to becoming better educated such that they can better discover what is most probably true about what is particular and general, idealized and non-idealized, and about both style and content, and without falling victim to mere rhetoric in our role as either an author or audience.

It can be extremely hard to recognize that an art of persuasion which helps our career can be bad for science and truth, by encouraging readers and listeners to accept what we advocate on insufficient grounds, namely by rhetoric instead of by ethics and weight of evidence. According to Plutarch and Shakespeare, Brutus was honest and wise, but Marc Antony won the day with his more emotional rhetoric directed at less educated citizens, and the Roman Republic fell.

We need more ethics, education, and character if our Republic is to survive the onslaught of increased rhetoric, especially when insufficiently supported by weight of evidence or merely by so-called "statistical studies" which in fact do not take all of the relevant variables which may be important into account or consideration. The standards of much science, especially in many or most of the social sciences, are not rigorous enough. Much more research into particulars as particulars is needed, that is, where causes as particularized influence acting at particular places and times as in realistic, that is, non-idealized semantics is primary.

INTRODUCTION

Professor: Do you want to know why you failed the examination with a zero?

Vera: No.

Prof: I will tell you anyway

Vera: To rub it in?

Prof: It wasn't a matter of evidence or truth.

Vera: I didn't think so.

Prof: Some veracity even stands out, but . . .

Vera: but . . .

Prof: This course is in the speech department.

Vera: Which is about rhetoric or the art of persuasion.

Prof: Yes, and since your grade depends on how well you persuade the rest of the students in the oral exam and me in the written part I am sorry to have to tell you . . .

Vera: I was not persuasive enough.

Prof: Do you know why?

Vera: Perhaps orally because I might have seemed to be lecturing the listeners about factual matters.

Prof: Exactly. You acted as if you were superior.

Vera: I might have accepted a low grade, but when given a zero it was clear that prejudice was at work.

Prof: Our reaction was human.

Vera: But not honorable.

Prof: This is not a class in ethics. You should learn how to influence people favorably as they are and not as you think they ought to be.

Vera: Which means taking advantage of their prejudices and irrational habits?

Prof: Precisely!

Vera: I cannot stoop that low.

Prof: Advertisers and politicians run the world, and they do it.

Vera: Not my world. I love truth first, last, and always, and refuse to mislead anyone just to "persuade" them.

Prof: And your essay was just as moralistic.

Vera: But it was you who graded the written part.

Prof: And I saw the same arrogant attitude.

Vera: Arrogant?

Prof: Yes, you criticized rhetoric instead of using it to persuade.

Vera: If I made factual errors, what were they?

Prof: Other things mattered more.

Vera: I understand. Did I fail your written test because I forgot to bring my pen and had to write with pencil?

Prof: Of course not. We are not influenced by trivia.

Vera: Because I alleged that truth mattered more than persuasion?

Prof: Not at all! Though failure to *persuade* us that truth was more important may have been a factor.

Vera: Because I claimed that mastering likely intent is more basic than understanding words?

Prof: No, not even in a speech class where words are primary.

Vera: Then why?

Prof: You failed the oral because of your obsession with "balanced" content which let your side of the argument down, and caused your team to lose the debate, which is also why they all thought you were trying to act superior.

Vera: And the written half?

Prof: Because you criticized my ideas.

Vera: I had to be honest and tell the truth.

Prof: Taking a position is a game, and you didn't play by the rules. Everyone knows that truth is relative and that persuasion matters most.

Vera: But I believe that truth comes first, and is not relative, though certainty may be.

Prof: This is not a course in belief, content, certainty, or truth.

Vera: But is rhetoric legitimate?

Prof: You failed to persuade us either way.

Vera: Perhaps you wanted more evidence and better argumentation.

Prof: Perhaps, if you could have improved or increased persuasion, hence you failed the course . . .

Vera: and with a zero.

Prof: and with a zero.

Vera: But since persuasion can be influenced by mere feeling and emotion which are not relevant . . .

Prof: But they *are* relevant and why rhetoric exists. If everyone were rational, then strong evidence and valid argumentation would be enough. Even "truth" might be enough.

Vera: Hence you think persuasion requires some kind of deception or one-sided presentation.

Prof: Often a lot.

Vera: But to deliberately mislead is immoral . . .

Prof: But often the only path to persuasion, and since it wins followers and votes and is the path to power, it is folly to reject it.

Vera: I don't believe that. Nor do I want power if the means are dirty.

Prof: Your essay was full of schoolmarmish "truth".

Vera: I thought that was pertinent.

Prof: No, it was impertinent because you failed to show sufficient respect for my ideas. Clever students write what their instructor wants to hear, or at least something which acknowledges its importance. This often persuades the teacher to give them a good mark.

Vera: I refuse to pander.

Prof: An essay or test is merely to make sure that a student has learned something from the teacher and his textbooks, but it is clear you learned nothing. And nothing plus nothing equals zero.

Vera: I cannot accept what I think is false.

Prof: Then fake it! That will persuade the teacher to give you something better.

Vera: I'm sorry. I cannot pretend to support a position I don't, even if it would win debating points, so honesty and truth are too important to be sacrificed for a good grade.

Prof: The only thing sacrificed is yourself.

Vera: If willingly done, can be fun.

Prof: If you can't win, then spin.

Vera: To cheat is moral defeat.

Prof: For a good grade, persuade.

Vera: I'm not afraid.

Prof: The social path avoids wrath.

Vera: If the "social" path means to be unduly pliant, then I prefer to be self-reliant.

Prof: Even in a speech class which teaches rhetoric and the art of persuading *other* people.

Vera: Isn't speech possible without deceiving *others*?

Prof: Speech without effect is pointless, and reason rarely persuades the irrational, but since we all have an emotional weak-point which rhetoric can find and fill, this give us a method to persuade, both the rational and the irrational to accept what is true.

Vera: But if rhetoric "works", to use an old pragmatic criterion for both meaning and truth, then you open the floodgates to all kinds of fraud and evil manipulation. You tempt the honorable to become dishonorable.

Prof: I only support rhetoric in the interest of truth.

Vera: And winning debates, as if persuasion mattered more.

Prof: Do you doubt my word?

Vera: No, only your support of rhetoric.

Prof: They are the same.

Vera: No they're not. Words, meaning, rhetoric, and truth are all different.

Prof: But interrelated in my understanding.

Vera: Maybe my "mistake" really was writing in pencil, as if I had no point and didn't care.

Prof: Do you have a point?

Vera: Yes, being honest.

Prof: And do you care?

Vera: Of course. I always want to learn.

Prof: But if so, then why did you challenge the legitimacy of rhetoric and the importance of persuasion?

Vera: Because I hoped to help raise *your* standards of honesty and truth.

Prof: With the aid of insults?

Vera: No. The truth cannot insult.

Prof: Even if it undermines my teaching?

Vera: Right.

Prof: Then why did you take the course?

Vera: At first, curiosity.

Prof: And then?

Vera: To expose the dark side of rhetoric: sly, slippery, and slanted. Plato's Socrates called it sophistry . . .

Prof: and Aristotle legitimate and necessary.

Vera: I also think it is hard to grade essays in a fair and responsible manner.

Prof: So now I'm irresponsible.

Vera: Everyone knows that grading essays can be willful and even arbitrary.

Prof: And you are sure of that?

Vera: No two professors agree. There is no objective standard. My zero could have been a hundred with a different teacher, especially if I had . . .

Prof: written the essay with a pen and not a pencil, I know.

Vera: But such "trivia" may influence some professors, even in the Speech Department".

Prof: Rubbish!

Vera: I prefer being honest to using spin.

Prof: You will never persuade anyone. Who do you think you are to lecture me? You prissy puritan!

Vera: But at least I will not be ashamed of myself.

Prof: Highminded fool!

Vera: Rhetoric is rubbish!

Prof: Get out now! Leave! Leave!.

Vera: Sayonara, immoralist!

Prof: Aufniemalssehen, plain Jane!

Chapter One

MEANING

Vera: I hope you can help me, Professor.

Frank: I will try.

Vera: You are an expert in semantics.

Frank: No, I am not. There are no experts. Semantics is about theory of meaning, and the word meaning "means" many different things, and they are not always compatible.

Vera: Who invented semantics?

Frank: "invent" may not be the right word. It was Frances Welby who introduced the term "semantics" into English in her translation of a book by the Frenchman Michel Bréal early in the 20th century, but it was her mother Lady Victoria Welby who began an analysis of the different meanings of the word "meaning" in order to help communication, especially among people with different intentions and assumptions.

Vera: What are some of those uses?

Frank: The verb to mean can "mean" to intend, to signify, to suggest, to imply, to indicate, to have value, and the noun form of "meaning" can "mean" intent, signification, significance, implication, importance, and value, and which are all related in some way to understanding or comprehension.

Vera: I am familiar with to mean as to intend and to signify, but could you give examples of the other uses?

Frank: "The sign means what it says." "Dark clouds often mean rain." "Your meaning escapes me." "That girl means a lot to me" and "What is the meaning of life?"

Vera: Okay, I get the point. "To mean" and "meaning" as both words and ideas are increasingly being used in new and additional ways, which in turn may well help inspire a proliferation of different types of semantics.

Frank: Furthermore, negative uses often suggest exaggerated criticism as if something cannot be understood which in fact can be understood but which we merely oppose. By suggesting the opposite of one or more of all of the different positive uses, terms such as "meaningless" and "nonsense" can function like virtually all-purpose opposition to condemn not only individual ideas or claims but whole fields, philosophies, or movements with a single word. No reasonable person uses or accepts such terror-terms which contribute so much to vast prejudgment.

Vera: but we are all unreasonable sometimes.

Frank: That is the problem.

Vera: I hate rhetoric.

Frank: It is simpler than using weight of evidence.

Vera: But less honorable.

Frank: No one can prove everything he says or writes, but we can often mention well-known supporting evidence or at least cite it, and qualification to match lack of evidence is an option, even for what seems naturally plausible. Best is normally research if we have the time or are willing to make the time, and if we love searching for truth, we will persevere.

Vera: If unclarified and unsupported by evidence then authors do often fall into using rhetoric.

Frank: Yes, Legitimate persuasion should be by weight of evidence.

Vera: What do you mean by evidence?

Frank: Some philosophers mean what can be made evident as if it could be directly sensed or made conscious to us.

Vera: And what do *you* mean?

Frank: I mean what most people mean, namely, what is generally meant in a court of law, either a relevant physical exhibit, relevant writing, measurement, photographs, or with certain qualifications relevant spoken testimony from witnesses.

Vera: So evidence has to be relevant?

Frank: Yes.

Vera: And true?

Frank: That is to be determined.

Vera: So false evidence can still be evidence?

Frank: If it is not yet known to be false.

Vera: And what is weight of evidence?

Frank: If after extensive research and careful judgment something seems probably true, then it constitutes weight of evidence.

Vera: And if new evidence is discovered or old evidence re-interpreted?

Frank: Then the weight of evidence could change, but as a rule if a great deal of evidence is collected and weighed, then one alternative will normally seem to prevail.

Vera: And if two or more alternatives still seem to have some support but without any option reaching beyond fifty percent, what should be done then?

Frank: More research should probably be carried out until one possibility seems highly probable and remains so even if research continues much further. On the other hand, one should naturally look for diverse kinds of relevant evidence from different people, places, times, and schools of thought.

Vera: But what if we don't have enough time to conduct a thorough examination?

Frank: The more important, the more research is normally needed.

Vera: But can't a single piece of evidence prove decisive?

Frank: It can be premature to count on it.

Vera: Do you have examples?

Frank: The weight of evidence for centuries seemed to be that all swans were white until black ones were discovered in Australia.

Vera: Does weight of evidence determine truth?

Frank: No. Correspondence with reality determines truth, but weight of evidence determines how probable we think it is that truth as correspondence with reality is the case.

Vera: So more evidence can change the weight?

Frank: Yes.

Vera: Can truth change?

Frank: No, but it can be hard to determine truth, and what we think is probably true can change.

Vera: I don't understand how information can add weight, or even the notion of weight itself.

Frank: Weight of evidence includes demonstration or what can be demonstrated; description and reports about description; comparisons and references to comparison. Also, some information is qualitatively more important, much more important, than other information, and hence weight of evidence does not necessarily reduce to mere preponderance of evidence. In difficult matters, individual items of information may have to be weighed separately for relevance and probable reliability. Thorough research can be a long process, and in a sense may never end. Like early votes in an election, early data is sometimes misleading and often weight can only be determined after discovering and trying to evaluate a great deal of evidence. Massive research and good judgment can be required.

Vera: Could you give examples?

Frank: Early maps showed California as an island, but more research gradually created enough weight of evidence to make it overwhelmingly probable that it was connected to the North American mainland.

Vera: In physical science one thinks of verification and falsification. Is the notion of weight of evidence still relevant there?

Frank: Yes. J.J. Thomson originally carried out experiments which seemed to indicate that electrons were waves, but when he repeated his experiments in a much more rigorous way, the weight of evidence began to indicate that they were particles.

Vera: So collecting more data using different methods and from a wider variety of sources can influence weight?

Frank: Yes, but it is still a qualitative notion which can require good judgment.

Vera: But in practice most of us do not literally present either evidence or weight of evidence but merely refer to its existence and accessibility. There is an element of trust involved.

Frank: That can be a problem, but weight of evidence can also be understood in a loose sense. For example, we all believe that lions and sharks are potentially dangerous, but we trust pictures and stories and the views of other people that they are indeed to be feared in certain situations. Hence, it seems reasonable to maintain that the weight of evidence is that many or most of them can be or are dangerous animals. In short, common sense relies heavily on weight of evidence, but often in a rather weak way which accepts common reports, opinions, pictures, beliefs as probably reliable. When strict accuracy becomes important or more important we tend to require more and better evidence and more careful judgment.

Vera: Poor common sense.

Frank: No, this is not a refutation of common sense, especially because most things we accept as probably true rest on a somewhat casual approach toward evidence. No one can carefully investigate everything, hence we normally have to think and act on the basis of what seems most likely in terms of the information we are already familiar with.

Vera: Why is evidence understood in law courts better than what philosophers mean by evidence?

Frank: It is not always better.

Vera: Why do *you* think it is better than identifying evidence merely with what is evident to the senses?

Frank: Because I think that much that happens which is never literally evident to anyone can still be real and relevant enough to be considered evidence by reasonable people whether in a court of law or not, in fact, with some qualifications even in philosophy. Ordinary people when in doubt normally appeal to dictionaries and encyclopedias, and even better, read more than one, since they sometimes disagree or change over time, though it can be unwise to always think that the latest version is more correct.

Vera: But is anything more certain than what we directly sense ourselves or than formal logic?

Frank: Yes, machine measurement is often more reliable and certain than eyeballing sensory appearances from a distance, and because formal logic is based on idealized meaning and idealized deduction, it is often better to rely on weight of evidence.

Vera: What does idealization mean?

Frank. Either to gild the lily or to simplify something so far that it distorts what is actually intended or understood or is the case about real persons and things at particular places and times.

Vera: What is the root meaning of meaning?

Frank: In Anglo-Saxon times to intend, a use which still survives in English and also in German when associated with or inferred from the verb "meinen".

Vera: Can you prove what was a common meaning of meaning as far back as unlettered Anglo-Saxon times?

Frank: We are not sure, since books in that language are few from then, pronunciation has changed, and later spelling. The large Oxford Dictionary based on historical methods quotes King Alfred from 888 A.D.

Vera: What was the main meaning of his verb?

Frank: To intend, at least according to English dictionaries which are big enough to mention probable origins.

Vera: What is the main use today?

Frank: The same in colloquial speech, to intend, but to mean as to signify has tended to obscure it in much written science and philosophy since those days, and even more recently other uses have sprouted as already mentioned before

Vera: I like the root and colloquial meaning *to intend*, since for an audience to understand what an author wants to communicate or is driving at we have to understand his intentions along with his most important assumptions. Hunting for likely intent can also expose and help us guard against being seduced by smooth talkers and rhetoric.

Frank: All rhetoric is not smooth, much is loud and emotional. Different audiences can be persuaded differently.

Vera: And a few not at all.

Frank: Meaning as intent seems more active and causal than meaning as if words could mean, since it is not clear how something like words by themselves could actually *do* anything.

Vera: Then what was the source?

Frank: Instead of saying "I use the word to convey my intent." the sentence was probably shortened increasingly over time to become "The word means intent" and then "The word signifies intent." In short, the passive object "word" gradually became treated as if it were an active subject of the sentence. Indeed, English has many nouns as grammatical objects which have become apparent subjects of sentences without them being or referring to anything active, which may be partly why the subject of a sentence in traditional grammar is sometimes regarded as referring to what does an action and sometimes merely to what the sentence is about. This ambiguity has cursed grammar since the Greeks.

Vera: This sounds speculative. Wasn't there a more concrete and likely explanation for why so many non-historians and non-psychologists switched from to mean as intend eventually to mean as signify?

Frank: Possibly because of the extensive use of spoken and written Latin in Medieval universities, which was a second language for almost everyone and almost equally foreign and difficult. Later, dictionaries appeared about vernacular languages like French and German, and of course English which tended to list socially approved significations plus in many cases the most common associations we make with words as if words literally mean or somehow could determine meaning. These developments have helped us adopt the habit of thinking that signification is the main meaning of meaning and that words, conventions, habits, and definitions are the most important variables in communication.

Vera: But if it is not true that meaning as signification is either logically, historically, or causally primary, then how have so many academics been able to preserve that view?

Frank: Partly because they look for necessary relations in an idealized context.

Vera: Is that wrong?

Frank: It can seem right in mathematical science, but if our primary concern is about truth or reality in the real, that is, the non-idealized world, then it is wrong.

Vera: I don't understand.

Frank: When we converse in a familiar, non-idealized language, then we don't notice the sound of words (if not too soft or loud) so much as link dictionary meaning with the sound, or we relate ideas, feelings, or action with the sound which seem most appropriate given the situation and what the user of the word most likely intends, expects, or is driving at.

Vera: And the result is communication?

Frank: Or a measure of it. Indeed, regardless of how a speaker or writer expresses himself, if an audience fails to understand what the author intends, assumes, or is driving at, then communication is incomplete or non-existent.

Vera: So using dictionary or so-called objective meaning cannot guarantee communication?

Frank: Right. And if they want more accurate and complete communication listeners normally ask: "What do *you* the author mean?" That is: "What are *you* driving at."

Vera: Okay. What *are* you driving at?"

Frank: That both dictionary meaning and the idealized meaning of logicians and mathematicians require the falsehood that symbols, words, sentences, and propositions mean independently of the intent and assumptions of real people expressing themselves at real places and times.

Vera: As if objective meaning were real?

Frank: Right.

Vera: And as if all science is idealized?

Frank: When in fact it is not.

Vera: Especially in history, psychology, observation, experiment, and much applied science?

Frank: Correct again.

Vera: And of course in the practical world.

Frank: In reality, people mean and not words, sentences, or "propositions"

Vera: What does language consist of?

Frank: Words, collocations, and sentences

Vera: Is meaning part of language?

Frank: It is often treated that way, especially when we distinguish between connotations and denotations.

Vera: Please explain that.

Frank: We commonly associate different types of meaning with words. Semantics studies those associations which seem to possess ideas or meaning, of which two kinds are called descriptive-connotation and value-connotation. Many words seem to have both. Because of the presence of value-connotation no language or meaning is fully objective.

Vera: But don't some people think language is objective?

Frank: Yes, and indeed, physically, spoken words are sound waves and written ones normally consist of ink or activated electronics, but these physical accompaniments are not normally what most people understand by either language or meaning.

Vera: They prefer something else?

Frank: Yes, people associate meaning with words, which is connotation, and in philosophy people use words to help suggest what they are referring to or driving at which they call denotation, and value connotation is present in much or most actual use of language.

Vera: But those factors are mental, though some philosophers seem to treat appearances and even ideas as physical.

Frank: And hopefully both mental referents and what seem to be physical are considered real, if they are capable of helping to influence other things.

Vera: But isn't the merely idealized or objectified also real?

Frank: As a mental process, yes, but what is idealized in the sense of being simplified too far is not fully real, and if simplified to the point of being totally fictional is unreal, and our understanding of both matter and mind is always mental.

Vera: But doesn't much science aim at simplicity?

Frank: We all want to save time and effort if it doesn't distort anything.

Vera: I mean logical or mathematical simplicity.

Frank: Abstract simplicity often simplifies too far.

Vera: So that it distorts what is real?

Frank: Alas, yes.

Vera: But what is more important formal logic or historical truth?

Frank: Sound philosophy must find a way to contain both.

Vera: In terms of pure or practical reason?

Frank: In terms of relevant weight of evidence to determine truth and both pure and practical reason.

Vera: Do you reject logic.

Frank: I favor pure reason, if based on non-idealized meaning.

Vera: Then it is no longer pure.

Frank: To suggest that logic based on real meaning is less pure than when based on idealized meaning is deceptive.

Vera: But isn't non-idealized meaning dependent on tools of practical reason like intent and assumption, mere psychological variables?

Frank: Yes, but many psychological factors seem real when abstract factors seem idealized or fictional as if less real or unreal. To the extent practical reason, including psychology, is needed to determine what is true I support it.

Vera: Even if contrary to science?

Frank: Even if contrary to idealized science.

Vera: So you believe that some science really is non-idealized?

Frank: Yes, especially much history and psychology.

Vera: Even if it relies on mere inductive logic, means-end logic, and cause-and-effect logic?

Frank: If properly qualified, yes.

Vera: Will that satisfy logicians and mathematicians?

Frank: It can satisfy those who distinguish between mind and matter, who study history and psychology extensively, and who put the search for non-idealized truth first.

Vera: Is semantics part of practical reason?

Frank: If it is reliable. then it is part of science.

Vera: Regardless of method?

Frank: If it is ethical, reliable, and genuinely practical, yes.

Vera: If most science is idealized, then your preference for what is non-idealized could be viewed as non- or anti-scientific.

Frank: Only by people who reject non-idealized science.

Vera: But many mathematicians think just that.

Frank: On reflection even they understand that observation and experimentation are important parts of science and that they are largely non-idealized types of procedure.

Vera: Perhaps as a means but not as an end. They want equations and scientific laws as if they define science.

Frank: Different scientists have different ends. Engineers, for example, often use equations, laws, and other abstractions as means to help further ends like building a bridge or inventing new electronic equipment.

Vera: I admit that our image of science as abstract equations and laws does not apply to all science and is not necessarily the chief concern of most scientists, But as long as that image prevails as defining science, then your defence of non-idealized research like in history and psychology is likely to be ignored or criticized, especially by many mathematicians and philosophers.

Frank: Science first developed as a rational search for truth as correspondence with reality. Neo-Scholastic tendencies as if idealized understanding were better, though often obscure or counterfactual is disappointing. Nevertheless, I accept that perspective as one way of understanding or attempting to do science, but I think those who idealize language, meaning, equations, or laws as if about idealized types of things under idealized conditions, should at least be fair and wise enough to acknowledge that those of us still concerned with truth as correspondence with reality, that is, with non-idealized particulars, should be willing to acknowledge that we are scientists and are also doing science.

Vera: I am not sure that they will ever be that tolerant, as long as the current image and the falsehood that all science is idealized prevails. Indeed, attempts to define science never include all of it, since no one knows all of it.

Frank: You are right and the prevailing image is one-sided, but some day more scientists themselves will realize it, and even accept that truth as non-idealized correspondence with reality remains a worthy and scientific goal.

Vera: Which came first: talking or writing?

Frank: All cultures seem to have learned to speak before learning to write, but dictionaries focus mostly on writing and almost always overlook tone of voice and value-connotation.

Vera: What is value-connotation?

Frank: Some words suggest something good or bad to listeners or readers, if they pay attention, but even if not, on a sub-conscious or unconscious level the value associations we make with words and expression can often still influence human judgment about what is true or false as well as good and bad. In rhetoric they are commonly used as a substitute for evidence.

Vera: Is value-connotation hard to change?

Frank: It an be very difficult, though ordinary connotation and denotation can often be re-defined for particular purposes, though whether new definitions will "stick" and be accepted by dictionaries is less certain. The problem is that because value-connotations are so tenacious as associations we make with words that if we use words in a different way or try to redefine them then we merely change the target of the good or bad connotation and do not really eliminate the value-connotation itself. In fact, many people who use rhetoric and not evidence to persuade often redefine words precisely in order to redirect good or bad value-connotations.

Vera: Are any value-connotations ever changed?

Frank: Yes.

Vera: Can you give me an example of shifting?

Frank: The names of cities are normally value-free, but Sodom and Gomorrah in the Ancient world, Chicago of the 1920's, and the Munich of 1938 usually carry bad-connotations, but with time most of these have become less prominent and may eventually disappear. Furthermore, value-connotation can vary to some extent with different audiences. For example, the expression "the rich" meaning rich people is likely to strike one political audience as neutral or good and another as negative or "bad"

Vera: What is connotation itself?

Frank: Most words, especially nouns, verbs, adjectives, and adverbs, have both connotations and denotations. Most mental associations we make with words are called "connotations" even if the mental associations are *about* something physical. In normal usage, however, the central or most important connotation is called the "denotation" of the word. In philosophy, however . . .

Vera: which I would like to avoid until I understand semantics better.

Frank: In philosophy, the word "denotation" does not mean the normal or most important connotation, but is associated with what words are alleged to refer to, which is usually outside of language.

Vera: Why use the qualification "alleged"?

Frank: Because in fact people do the referring and not words.

Vera: Because words are almost always passive and rather impotent?

Frank: Yes, as we mentioned before. We can use words to try to do things, but by themselves words as mere expressions tend to have a very limited causal capacity to act in terms of influence.

Vera: But you still think that most value-connotation is hard to change?

Frank: I was thinking of words with a long history of bad connotations for almost everyone such as "stealing" or "treason" or on the good side "friendly" and "helpful".

Vera: Can't those words also be re-defined?

Frank: If words consist of denotations plus strong value connotations, then the former yes and the latter normally no.

Vera: But most words if they have value connotations at all have much weaker ones than "stealing" or "treason".

 Frank: But if weak and largely overlooked, then value-connotation is often more effective as a tool of rhetoric, that is, of persuasion under-supported by evidence.

Vera: What is common sense?

Frank: The practical person's best understanding.

Vera: What does it rest on?

Frank: Mostly experience, proverbs, and conversation, but also some schooling and use of dictionaries, encyclopedias, and news sources

Vera: Why do so many intellectuals criticize it?

Frank: Because they misunderstand it as if it were merely a primitive stage before science.

Vera: What else are they overlooking?

Frank: That proverbs are normally centuries old, rarely change, still apply to most current problems, and are often more reliable than most social and intellectual fashions.

Vera: Are most intellectuals and scientists practical?

Frank: They often think they are.

Vera: Why is persuasion necessary if common sense can solve most everyday problems?

Frank: It is precisely when common sense cannot solve something that persuasion may be necessary, which often means that persuasion should normally attempt to employ a higher standard of evidence like measurement or demonstration.

Vera: And if persuasion is used to overcome resistance or disagreement without any accompanying evidence?

Frank: Then it should fail.

Vera: But if it succeeds?

Frank: Then it is rhetoric.

Vera: Which is normally bad.

Frank: Almost always, but it has its uses, and is sometimes hard to avoid.

Vera: I reject it as dishonorable.

Frank: Even in emergencies?

Vera: If I want to persuade I will use evidence.

Frank: Good, at least normally.

Vera: One thing more. If rhetoric can help us persuade other people without using or referring to evidence, then why is it successful so often?

Frank: Because readers and especially listeners are often unconsciously influenced by the value-connotations of words and the way they are expressed. Or put differently, the use of words having "good" or "bad" connotations can encourage premature belief.

Vera: Is prejudgment the same as prejudice?

Frank: Originally. And to some extent still today, but any belief or strongly held idea can be called a prejudice if the degree of belief is stronger than the weight of evidence or is held in an unreasonably tenacious manner. Dogmatism is a kind of prejudice, but most belief if capable of being changed by evidence is not prejudice.

Vera: I guess prejudgment is bad because we shouldn't believe something before we have checked the evidence, but it is sometimes hard not to, especially if we have read something else by the same author or heard a similar argument from him of from his friends or allies.

Frank: For the benefit of any one who still has a low opinion of proverbs or who doesn't understand that they are not universal truths but only hold for particular situations where they can be very important, there are even proverbs about the danger of prejudgment.

Vera: Really? I didn't know that.

Frank: For example: "You can't tell a book by its cover." And related proverbs: "Better be sure than sorry." "Don't cross a bridge till you get there." and "Discretion is the better part of valor"

 Vera: I like the proverb: "Do as I say, not as I do."

Frank: The relation of rhetoric to prejudgment is a close one, since it is hearing or reading rhetoric which often helps cause prejudgment.

Vera: With the assistance of the value-connotation of words ?

Frank: Yes. If a word sounds good, then unwittingly we often lean toward what the word is used to help refer to, and if bad, then the opposite, though of course the actual psychological situation can be much more complex. It is human reaction to hearing, reading, and value connotation and not to words themselves which seem to help influence or provoke the resulting prejudgment, and unfortunately much of the reaction is not fully conscious to us. Many people are persuaded by rhetoric until they think about what was actually said and probably intended.

Vera: Unfortunately, almost everyone has emotional or mental weak points which clever users of rhetoric and value-judgment can find and exploit.

Frank: Right. Such a tempter or temptress who says what you want to hear or in a congenial manner or tone of voice.

Vera: He may soar or soft-soap, make you feel his feeling, or challenge his listeners to follow him. He can be an orator or a Pied Piper, a plain man like Marc Antony. . .

Frank: or a dynamic politician or man of action, a leader like Napoleon, Hitler, Stalin, or Mao.

Vera: I decline to be led. Why do you object to the notion that "words mean" when rhetoric seems to prove the contrary?

Frank: Meaning in a third sense may indeed suggest a kind of causal implication as in "Dark clouds mean rain", nor is rhetoric as a process a kind of natural or irresistible force. Words do seem to mean as signification even if it is misleading by overlooking that in fact people make associations with words and use words to mean in the sense of intend, refer, or assume.

Vera: What is the difference between language and meaning?

Frank: The use of language as words and understandable combinations of them is a common way to suggest meaning, especially normal meaning, but it is not the only way, since gestures and tone of voice can help or even take precedence in suggesting ideas or meaning.

Vera: Can language determine meaning?

Frank: No, but there are many strong habits of association.

Vera: Does language include tone of voice?

Frank: Spoken language does and even written dialogue can suggest it.

Vera: Is value-connotation part of meaning and language?

Frank: Yes, and can refute the claim that all language and meaning are objective.

Vera: As in much irony, satire, and prejudgment?

Frank: Those too. And when put in quotation marks to suggest doubt or reservation.

Vera: But isn't that going stylistically out of fashion?

Frank: I distinguish between science and style, prefer descriptive to prescriptive grammar, and emphasize that selective tone of voice, irony, satire, humor, analogy, and non-literal meaning are more common than the use of pure dictionary meaning in most human conversation. As for employing redefinition and value-connotation to help cause prejudgment by other people, while most people would reject the practice if brought to their attention, nevertheless, appear to unwittingly practice it a lot.

Vera: Research often takes too much time. It is easier to pre-condemn everything unfamiliar or which has a bad connotation.

Frank: Unless truth really matters.

Vera: If meaning and language were truly objective, would they still exclude value-connotation and prejudgment?

Frank: Counterfactual questions can be hard to answer. Were it possible for meaning and language to be objective, then yes, but if not, then no. But I fear you miss the point. Meaning and expression even without associated value-connotation and resulting prejudgment might still seem objective without really being objective.

Vera: I see. Both apparent and real objectivity can often help persuade, especially with educated people who are less vulnerable to blatant emotional persuasion, but both are forms of rhetoric or mere promissory notes when unaccompanied by weight of evidence. Nor can everyone fulfill her promises.

Frank: Yes, Attractive form or style like soft-soaping which it often partly resembles can also be a form of spin or rhetoric. But to repeat: All rhetoric is not misleading or immoral. It may sometimes be more important to rouse citizens to a good cause, than simply to tell the truth in either a persuasive or unpersuasive way.

Vera: I disagree! We need wise precedent for the future more than mere opportunistic or undeserved success.

Frank: Under normal circumstances, yes. But perhaps the most seductive of all rhetoric is to oppose it in principle while inconspicuously using it in practice.

Vera: Sometimes, dear example, it is hard not to be emotional against emotion, prejudiced against prejudice, and rhetorical against rhetoric, but I still don't like it!

Frank: Don't worry, truth is not changed by you or other people sharing the same faults, though many people think otherwise.

Vera: Shouldn't you be trying harder to express your best understanding of what is true, real, and right?

Frank: I don't always know what it is.

Vera: But shouldn't you say what you mean?

Frank: I can't always do that either. We all normally mean and assume more than we can easily express.

Vera: Or sometimes want to express?

Frank: Furthermore, since different languages can be used to suggest virtually the same meaning, it is clear that language is different from meaning and does not determine meaning, but that human intent, reference, and assumptions do.

Vera: Good. You did mean what you said, but did not say .. ,

Frank: all I mean.

Vera: What does that mean?

Frank: As seem to imply? That it can be hard to reach ideal goals. Indeed, while tone of voice can often help children infer meaning when we are young, a speaker's mental rhythm and tone of voice can also help listeners catch intended meaning after we have forgotten the words themselves.

Vera: Why don't dictionaries explain that?

Frank: Because many editors and linguists still think that words mean, that dictionaries and conventions determine meaning, that all meaning is objective, and that mental rhythm, tone of voice, value-connotation, and meaning as intent are irrelevant.

Vera: Many mothers recite out loud from books to help their children understand.

Frank: Part of the problem is indeed the false opinion that written language is more basic than spoken language.

Frank: I agree, and rhythmic sound like rhyming poetry can make words, music, and verse easier to remember.

Vera: But aren't some scholars tone deaf?

Frank: Most react to loud criticism.

Vera: What is reference?

Frank: Something words are alleged to do and what particular persons actually do.

Vera: Is it a process or relation?

Frank: It can usually be understood either way, but incompletely and for different purposes.

Vera: Does reference imply the existence of what is referred to?

Frank: In some types of formal logic, yes, but not in the real or non-idealized world.

Vera: What are assumptions?

Frank: Ideas we normally take for granted.

Vera: Then why not try to change them for the better?

Frank: If more people would try to discover what their own assumptions are, analyze them, and try to improve upon them, then we would have more genuine philosophers.

Vera: Who might still disagree with each other?

Frank: Different goals, different depths of introspection, and reading different books or in a different order often lead to different beliefs and preferences.

Vera: Is philosophical agreement possible?

Frank: Yes. It is easy for the superficial to follow the same fashion.

Vera: But can't deep minds also agree?

Frank: If thinkers study the full range of very different philosophies and analyze their own assumptions and the assumptions underlying them, then they might be attracted to the same foundation theory.

Vera: That sounds very conditional and hypothetical.

Frank: It was not hypothetical that Bacon and Descartes rejected much Scholastic philosophy based on formal logic and idealized meaning, and in the process both giants suggested ways to bring common sense, science, and philosophy into closer compatibility with each other.

Vera: Which Berkeley, Hume, and Kant rejected?

Frank: And worse than presentism, we have seen a restoration of Scholastic ways of thinking among many recent logicians, mathematicians, and some mathematical scientists.

Vera: Do we need a new scientific revolution?

Frank: Not if we still accept heliocentrism, atomism, and the representational theory of perception.

Vera: As theories or probable truths?

Frank: If the weight of evidence still supports that the planets revolve round the sun and not the earth, that mental representations of external objects are still different from those objects, and if atoms and molecules still exist, then regardless of how physical science changes in other respects, then it still rests primarily on the initial Scientific Revolution.

Vera: But many philosophers reject all three now, even though their sensory or presentist theories about matter cannot keep out most intrusive mental distortion, like representism can.

Frank: Which suggests that we need a new philosophical revolution which makes a more lasting effort to bring history, psychology, physical science, and common sense together.

Vera: But wouldn't it be eclectic?

Frank: Perhaps to some extent, but indirect realism and mind-matter dualism are already widely accepted by most influence-focused thinkers now, and to demand a completely deductive and hence idealized system from the incomplete and largely inductive capacity of finite and fallible human beings is neither reasonable nor practical in either science or philosophy.

Vera: Which do you prefer? Common sense as Locke's indirect realism or Reid's direct realism, since both men have been called common sense philosophers?

Frank: I think Locke came closer to the indirect realism of Galileo, Newton, and the mature Planck, and Einstein.

Vera: Your answer sounds plausible, at least for a historian, but I refuse to be easily persuaded about basic matters.

Frank: Good! One should look before . . .

Vera: leaping? How quaint. You really do like proverbs.

Frank: Unlike most intellectuals, I actually examined them.

Vera: And they never forgave you? Did they?

Frank: I trust proverbs more than most philosophy.

Vera: If the proverbs are applied to the most suitable problems.

Frank: Double-domes have a lot to learn from them.

Vera: Maybe I do too.

Frank: Let us both learn more from history and proverbs. There was often something better in the past.

Vera: Like Newtonian mechanics?

Frank: No! The issue is not simple.

Vera: Or Newton's indirect epistemology?

Frank: Yes, but we must untangle them, since many recent philosophers try to justify rejecting the latter on grounds taken from problems about the former.

Vera: And that is not legitimate?

Frank: I don't think it follows or is true.

Vera: How is it relevant to semantics?

Frank: Because my opponents believe in objective meaning where it neither exists nor is properly relevant. But please let me give a historical explanation of a disconnect between science and philosophy.

Vera: I will try to stay awake long enough.

Frank: Descartes' physics did seem half-mechanistic as if nature were a plenum full of inertia and push-pull behavior, but his indirect philosophy and that of Newton and Locke allowed for inertia, magnetism, electricity, gravitation, and other non-mechanistic action, like much mental and other human behavior.

Vera: Then why is Newtonian mechanics so closely associated with mechanistic science?

Frank: Through misunderstanding, and subsequently, because Newton had not yet successfully anticipated later detailed research discoveries about heat, electricity, magnetism, and other microscopic and sub-atomic behavior, *and philosophically*, because opponents of Newtonian representism and mind-matter dualism like Ernst Mach tried to give the impression that physical science was only concerned with describing and relating appearances, even if Einstein was initially influenced by that view, which misrepresented Newton's indirect epistemology.

Vera: What about Einstein's refutation of Newton's absolutes?

Frank: His refutation was based on the notion that light can influence space and time, especially if light is regarded as a necessary factor in physical measurement, but were it possible to measure space, time, plus matter and motion without using or presupposing light, then Newtonian space, time, motion, place, and rest might still be regarded as real and absolute as they often were before Einstein.

Vera: Even you cannot persuade me without more evidence. Retaining Newtonian mechanics is too radical.

Frank: I am not retaining Newtonian mechanics as something unrefuted, even if it is still regarded as a limiting case, but Newton's indirect and largely representist epistemology.

Vera: And many navigators still use geocentric astronomy. Does that make it true, better, or superior to more recent theory?

Frank: Their work is often more useful and understandable.

Vera: You carry non-idealized science too far.

Frank: Its just valid common sense. If history and applied science solve a problem better than what is more abstract, idealized or harder to understand, then obviously . . .

Vera: Nothing is really obvious. And I will not see modern science scorned in this way.

Frank: I do not scorn anything, and I agree that nothing is true just because someone says so.

Vera: I will reflect on and may accept later what many people manifestly reject now. To challenge sacred beliefs in science or religion requires extensive proof and not a mere dialogue.

Frank: If nothing is unconditionally certain, then no proof is more than probable. Hence, one should not be afraid to consider and learn from other points of view, regardless of how shocking or unexpected.

Vera; I am not afraid.

Frank: That's a good girl.

Vera: Still, I'm not ready to accept Newtonian philosophy, and please stop patronizing me, even if your intentions are honorable, and even if Galileo, Planck, and Einstein also accepted a consciously indirect world view.

Frank: All persuasion is not rhetoric, and all praise is not patronizing.

Vera: You talk about weight of evidence, but show precious little.

Frank: Okay. I will demonstrate the result of weight of evidence, field by field. In *archeology* Schliemann and subsequent researchers have proved that the existence of Troy was more than a myth. In *astronomy*, the discovery of parallax and ability to use the heliocentric theory to explain the apparent retrograde motion of the planets proved that the planets revolve around the sun. In *biology*, digging up the remains of dead mammoths has proved that they once roamed parts of the frozen North. In *chemistry*, careful use of electron microscopes has proved that molecules exist, and more recently we have even photographed atoms.

Vera: Okay! Okay! But where does "weight of evidence" affect semantics and rhetoric?

Frank: When we forget the *meanings* we normally associate with words we look them up in a dictionary. When we forget *words* themselves but remember ideas and meaning we usually look the words and synonyms up in a thesaurus. Forgetting and finding are normally understood as mental behavior, and neither could take place unless we also had mental awareness of meanings and words, that is, their subjective capacity in our mind or brain. Words as sound waves or ink on paper are physical and objective, but they are not the same thing as real words in terms of mental awareness of them. Similarly, meaning is not the word "meaning" and is not determined by it. Rather, human beings identify meaning with an aspect of human understanding whose existence can often be made conscious to us with the use of linguistic expression as in dictionaries and even without linguistic expression as when we try to find a word but already have the meaning or idea in mind.

Vera: This is theory, not weight of evidence.

Frank: Older people, including myself, often forget words but remember meaning. Both psychological and physiological testing has proved this. I have taken such tests, and remember the results. I think this comes very close to weight of evidence.

Vera: Being close does not always count for much in science.

Frank: On the contrary, testing results in many sciences come within plus or minus degrees. Close can be very important.

Vera: Physically close and approximately close in terms of relative certainty are two different things.

Frank: True, but most sciences use both physical closeness and closeness as relative or comparative certainty. One can hardly be totally exact in either case. And . . .

Vera: Please don't rush me! Couldn't your opponents still be right about philosophy even if their semantics is wrong?

Frank: I think it is improbable, given the weight of evidence we have just presented.

Vera: Why not?

Frank: Because they often prefer simplicity and a measure of idealization to probable truth about real things and processes, that is, what actually exists. Even many historians of science seem unaware that Newton's science is not refuted by the mere absence of sensory and conscious relations. Why not? Because Newton like Galileo, the mature Planck, and Einstein, and most indirect realists consider what is physical to be logically independent of and beyond all mere sensory and conscious relations of the kind Mach identified with science. Einstein was young when he misunderstood Mach, but later realized that what Newton identified with absolute space, time, motion, place, and rest could be influenced by physical light in a way which had nothing to do with Mach's presentist arguments.

Vera: Please stop criticizing your scientific betters.

Frank: If what I say is false, then please refute me.

Vera: You have enough enemies, and don't need me to pile on. Furthermore, when all is said and done, I may actually be on your side.

Frank: I appreciate that.

Vera: Is semantics more about meaning or persuasion?

Frank: Both. Without meaning there is no persuasion.

Vera: But shouldn't the right feelings help?

Frank: Weight of evidence ought to be sufficient.

Vera: And if insufficient or absent, there is still rhetoric and feeling? And aren't they often bad?

Frank: Often very bad. Indeed, honorable speakers and writers feel an obligation *not* to deceive or mislead.

Vera: What if an advocate believes his own rhetoric?

Frank: Then he should include the evidence which persuaded him and not just emote or spout.

Vera: Are rhetoric and propaganda the same?

Frank: They are similar in many ways, but there are some differences.

Vera: Such as?

Frank: If propaganda is concealed and includes little or no evidence, then it can be called "rhetoric", but much propaganda is open support for a particular position or cause and is supported by evidence.

Vera: Then rhetoric is worse than propaganda?

Frank: From an ethical point of view, it can be when deliberately deceptive, but propaganda is often on a very large scale, and because one-sided, even if it uses evidence and often tells the truth can still be misleading and even more dangerous with more people.

Vera: But is it always possible or wise to only use neutral words and present more than one side of an argument?

Frank: Neutral words may conceal unneutral beliefs and aims, and there are so many sides to many arguments, that even presenting two sides can be unfair, especially if one is a strawman or we use invidious distinctions, like comparing science and metaphysics, as if science were good and metaphysics bad, when in fact as ontology or part of foundation theory is metaphysics, is truly fundamental, and all scientists have some foundation assumptions, whether they realize it or not.

Vera: I can only think of trying harder to be fair and use ordinary words, clarify our intentions and assumptions, and add evidence or at least words used to refer to evidence.

Frank: Clarification can take a lot of time and surprisingly an excess can sometimes interfere with communication and persuasion. To repeat, if author and audience share the same underlying aims and assumptions this normally helps a lot, but when different, in spite of other precautions, miscommunication is likely to happen, even with surface agreement.

Vera: Why?

Frank: Because most assumptions consist of overlooked things which we normally take for granted, which can vary a lot from person to person.

Vera: No one can say all he means.

Frank: People who think appearances are the real external physical world do not mean the same thing by physical objects as people who think appearances are mental and merely represent the external physical world, and these differences are almost never mentioned in dictionaries.

Vera: So philosophical differences can make communication more difficult?

Frank: Yes, but that is merely one example of where assumptions are a serious problem, especially if people want to communicate or understand more than one thing from their partners.

Vera: How can we communicate when aims and assumptions are different and largely unconscious on both sides?

Frank: If we have the time, we can start by trying to make more of what we usually take for granted conscious as well as study the likely assumptions of ourselves and other people.

Vera: But if we don't have the time or interest for full communication, and the normal use of words by an author is not enough to communicate much, because of philosophy, different aims and assumptions, and because of unusual circumstances and people, then how *does* accurate and full communication happen?

Frank: Often it doesn't, and since author and audience are normally looking for communication only about a single thing, they can often endure miscommunication about everything else.

Vera: Wow!

Frank: When either party wants to communicate or understand more accurately or more fully, then it is here that the responsibility of both parties but especially of an audience for increasing or completing communication can become important, especially when the author is dead, inaccessible, lazy, or simply doesn't try very hard, then readers and listeners can help.

Vera: How?

Frank: by focusing on likely intent and relevant assumptions.

Vera: But while I hate rhetoric and especially concealed purposes which can help mislead, I still don't want to tell everyone all my plans.

Frank: True, we all sometimes want to conceal some of our own motives and some of our intentions, but without being devious or misleading anyone.

Vera; Right, if we are honest and hate rhetoric.

Frank: I will mention a puzzle, and please look for an answer. If a scholar tries to understand an old document written in a foreign language and especially in an earlier version of that, what should he do?

Vera: What can he do? Except study the old language and try to discover who the author was and what he most likely intended and wanted to communicate or was driving at.

Frank: Correct. But here you see a different kind of meaning at work, one which will seem more subjective to many people and much more difficult to be certain about. A responsible author tries to use normal words and normal meaning, that is, meaning as signification, but since he also takes a lot for granted which he does not express, then communication often fails, especially when each side or party take different things for granted or have other expectations, but if the audience still cannot understand because of differences in philosophical or other assumptions or for other reasons, but still wants to understand more, then an audience can change focus from words and what they allegedly mean to people and what they probably mean, that is, switch from meaning as signification to meaning as intent, difficult as it often is to pin down the latter accurately and with fairness.

Vera: But is understanding meaning as intent only important for audiences?

Frank: It might seem so, but a wise author, because of differences in underlying assumptions, will try to clarify some of his own intentions and those of other people in his own mind before speaking or writing.

Vera: I agree that it is usually more important for an audience to focus on the likely intentions and assumptions of authors to help protect readers and listeners from rhetoric and premature persuasion.

Frank: But it can be so hard or seemingly unnecessary to accurately understand motives and intentions that some audiences don't even try.

Vera: Which invites even more rhetoric from unscrupulous speakers and writers.

Frank: That is precisely what happens, when logicians, mathematicians, and others who believe in objective language or objective meaning refuse to focus on what other people intend, or they try to logically deduce meaning merely from what is expressed. They fail to understand not only the many differences between literal and figurative meaning and of course irony, satire, facetiousness, and jokes, but become putty in the paws of any clever rascal gifted at rhetoric or persuasion.

Vera: And even if an audience understands each word in a sentence it may still miss the author's point.

Frank: Right, hence to understand more, then believers in objective meaning need to change their position in order to become less narrow and gullible.

Vera: But don't most audiences, even logicians and mathematicians, naturally want to understand as much as possible?

Frank: No. Economy of effort and time can matter more to them than accurate or full communication. Brevity may be the soul of wit, but depth of understanding is almost always more important. Furthermore, as quick thinkers many think that they already know what speakers and writers want to communicate anyhow, so why waste time listening or reading? Furthermore, miscommunication can happen even in the most familiar language.

Vera: So we have to understand two types of semantics, what words mean and what people mean?

Frank: Yes, and getting at what particular authors mean is ultimately more basic if communication is to be as accurate and complete as possible, especially about documents and books, but also in science and in everyday life.

Vera: Is what different parties take for granted part of intent?

Frank: As an assumption or more than one, sometimes yes and sometimes no. If an assumption is also a belief it can be very relevant, but many assumptions have rarely if ever been made conscious, and if conscious it is not always certain whether they would be accepted as a person's belief. In rational terms, we should only believe as strongly as the weight of evidence justifies after research is made as relevant and exhaustive as feasible, and if something seems more improbable than probable and we admit it, then alleged belief as a kind of hope, intent, or wishful thinking is not real belief.

Vera: Oh my God, semantics and philosophy can each be difficult. Everyone takes so many different things for granted, that even sharing the same vocabulary may not help much.

Frank: Which can mean in the sense of *implication* a third meaning of meaning.

Vera: Oh dear! And we haven't even mentioned that both parties can believe and act as if communication exists when it doesn't, or not on a fundamental level.

 Frank: Furthermore, the dictionary-inspired belief that meaning is what words mean can make it more difficult for most people to realize that meaning as intent and assumption are in fact more fundamental than meaning as signification, that is, than word or literal sentence meaning and that events or logic can also mean, not as words or intent but as alleged or actual implication.

Vera: What is "alleged implication"?

Frank: What seems to necessarily follow as formal or logical deduction, but may or does not.

Vera: Does anything "necessarily follow" in fact?

Frank: If one idealizes language and meaning, the notion can seem valid.

Vera: But without being valid "in the real world"?

Frank: Right. There is no unconditional necessity in non-idealized nature or for finite and fallible human beings.

Vera: But we can come so close that it is hardly practical to deny it.

Frank: We all claim that many things are certain or necessary, but almost never mean unconditional certainty or unconditional necessity.

Vera: Is anything unconditionally the case?

Frank: Probably not in a strict sense, because if proof is really proof it must be unconditional, but we can always find relevant conditions. Even Cartesian certainty "I think therefore I exist", and nothing seems more certain than that for most people, rests on conditions: First, that doubting is a form of thinking, when we often mean a situation is in doubt even if no one thinks that; second, that all thinking has a thinker; third, that "I" am that thinker; fourth, that the term "I" is unambiguous, and fifth, that in spite of Descartes' mention of a demon who undoes logic Descartes still seems to presuppose that logic is still applicable.

Vera: Which you reject?

Frank: On the contrary, I agree with his conclusion and with many of his assumptions, but I merely want to point out that he does use many assumptions which condition the truth of his conclusion, such that even if almost certainly true, his conclusion is not unconditionally true.

Vera: So there is no absolute proof?

Frank: Not in an unconditional sense

Vera: But there is truth "beyond a reasonable doubt"?

Frank: Yes, but the emphasis should be on reasonable.

Vera: So everything rational is not reasonable?

Frank: Right. Many philosophers and even some scientists have alleged that because of alleged infinities or apparent infinite regresses, which are supposedly *rational* concepts, that therefore something is factually impossible, such as Aristotle reasoned against atoms, Spinoza against starting from other than "self-evidence", and the notion that dividing something by zero results in what is infinite. But if we assume that common sense in the form of weight of evidence is more *reasonable*, then we will admit that atoms are probably real, that sound reasoning and true results can start from something else than "self-evidence", and that many mathematical infinities can be circumvented in a practical way with some form of what physicists call "renormalization".

Vera: Can it be rational to exaggerate?

Frank: Not within its own context of assumptions.

Vera: Is to intend to exaggerate?

Frank: Not exactly. But to express without intended qualification can seem to exaggerate.

Vera: Unless meaning is objective?

Frank: You still cling to . . .

Vera: but logic is important, even if idealized! Can't we extend honest meaning by getting at what words or propositions imply? Your third kind of meaning?

Frank: In a way, yes, but since what authors actually intend, refer to, assume, or believe is not always what seem to be implied in a rigorous deductive sense, then they risk putting words in other people's mouths and insisting they mean what they deny meaning or intending to mean, which from our point of view can be conditional proof of miscommunication or bad intent on their part, and perhaps a sign that they really don't want to understand what a speaker or writer actually means, a discovery which can make them angry as well.

Vera: So everything rational is not always reasonable?

Frank: Not if we take factual or practical factors into account.

Vera: Does factual mean "sensory"

Frank: For Ernst Mach and some phenomenalists it does.

Vera: But not for you?

Frank: I think that everything true or real is factual, but not in Mach's sense where only sensations are facts or factual.

Vera: But you think that none of that is "unconditionally certain"?

Frank: When we use words like true, real, certain, fact, and valid, I think we should always intend qualification, and if the conditional nature of our understanding is likely to be overlooked, then we should express qualification.

Vera: What if a claim is universal like in some mathematical science, such that private intent and "qualification" do not matter?

Frank: They still matter if accurate, and full communication and truth as correspondence with reality also matter.

 Vera: And if universal claims and scientific laws transcend conditionality and the need for qualification?

Frank: Then the claims and the laws are both speculative.

Vera: Like semantics?

Frank: Some semantic theories are speculative, especially attempts to objectify language and idealize meaning or who think that all rhetoric is legitimate and who also narrow and slant basic classification in philosophy as if all *other* points of view were "metaphysical", "psychologistic", or "meaningless".

Vera: What have *you* ever done to make language and meaning more fair and less prejudicial?

Frank: I have tried to emphasize the destructive effect which the value-connotation of *basic classification* in all fields and movements, but especially in semantics and philosophy, have done. Terms like "metaphysics", "psychologism", and "meaningless" or "nonsense" should not be used in basic classification or to defend it against criticism.

Vera: Could you give *positive* examples?

Frank: I replace the pejorative terms "metaphysical" with "consciously indirect", "psychologistic" with mental, and "meaningless" with hard to understand.

Vera: More examples, please:

Frank: I also distinguish between direct and indirect realism and "idea-lism as sensory or conscious presentism from "ideal-ism" as love of hope or high ideals. My basic classification in philosophy as foundation theory is between what can be made consciously direct and what cannot, with the first called "presentism" and the second an indirect position or "representism".

Vera: Won't many philosophers still oppose your attempt to employ more fair and inclusive classification, even if yours actually were less prejudicial?

Frank: Yes, because proof and refutation in terms of one person's underlying aims and assumptions normally will not persuade another person with different goals and assumptions.

Vera: Unless one or both parties use rhetoric or pretend that language or meaning is objective when it is not?

Frank: And conceal their own assumptions or the diversity of different points of view.

Vera: Is all semantics philosophical?

Frank: No, But a deeper understanding of it is.

Vera: Maybe I am not ready for that yet.

Frank: Even most philosophers misunderstand other philosophy, so please don't worry about the problem at this stage.

Vera: Why do you say that?

Frank: Many philosophers seem more concerned about formal logic and valid deduction than about truth, reality, qualification, or weight of evidence.

Vera: And is their preference wrong?

Frank: It is short-sighted.

Vera: What is wrong with logic?

Frank: Nothing is wrong with logic based on realistic meaning and non-idealized understanding.

Vera? What do you mean?

Frank: Formal logic rests on objectified language and the alleged meaning of words, symbols, and propositions which idealize meaning at best and falsify it at worst

Vera: So?

Frank: Real language is not objective and real meaning is in the intent and assumptions of real persons at particular places and times.

Vera: But if logic does not use objective language and meaning, then it becomes ambiguous.

Frank: Formal logic is more ambiguous precisely because neither language nor meaning are really objective.

Vera: Don't philosophers and logicians have a right to idealize and use their own definitions?

Frank: In terms of freedom of thought and speech, yes, but not in terms of ethics, if what they are doing is deliberately misleading or false.

Vera: Is it okay to use reason to support what is irrational?

Frank. No. That is called "apologetics" and is especially shameful in a world where weight of evidence and extensive qualification should prevail.

Vera: Many religious people may take offence.

Frank: Wise religion emphasizes hope, not over-belief.

Vera: Do you also object to Islamist laws against free speech, maltreatment of minorities, rejection of apostasy and opposition to separation of church and state?

Frank: I don't agree with any form of over-belief, but I also favor free speech and democratic government, but not a right to be irrational.

Vera: How can you of all people favor religion?

Frank: By hoping instead of over-believing.

Vera: If science is too objective and religion too subjective, then what is left?

Frank: Relative objectivity about both matter and mind remain, that is, about both the genuinely objective world, and honest and accurate historical description of the mental world.

Vera: Language may be subjective, but it is not always best understood merely as a historical process.

Frank: Right. Language without meaning is not language, and if meaning is in the intent and assumptions of real speakers and writers, then it is subjective in a good sense and not objective, even according to the deepest understanding of most opponents.

Vera: But can't dictionaries and conventions still make language and meaning partly objective?

Frank: Not really. We often treat them as if they were partly or wholly objective, but if people write dictionaries and form conventions, and people can be influenced by mental and hence subjective factors like thinking, believing, feeling, and prejudging, then neither language nor meaning as aids to communication are significantly objective, except in a merely relative or comparative way.

Vera: Oh dear! If logic and philosophy are not objective or do not rest on objective language and meaning, then formal logic may not be the most important factor in philosophy.

Frank: At least not logic which rests on objectified language and idealized meaning.

Vera: Then what is most important in philosophy?

Frank: Non-idealized searching for the most profound understanding and truth.

Vera: Is there a name for that?

Frank: Yes. *Basic Inquiry.*

Vera: How close is that to inquisition?

Frank: It is a self-deepening form of introspection.

Vera: How would we have to understand language to make it an *objective* tool of introspection?

Frank: I don't think it can be done! Introspection is subjective.

Vera: And should not even be attempted?

Frank: How can I answer? Like Socrates, I cannot honestly claim to be unconditionally certain of anything, and like Arcesilaus, I cannot even claim to be unconditionally certain of that, but I do think that introspection as self-analysis has value, especially when it can help us discover assumptions and presuppositions which we had not been aware of before

Vera: But if it were possible to make self-analysis objective how would it have to be attempted?

Frank: To make language or introspection objective in a strict or absolute sense, we would probably have to blur all distinctions between mind and matter and between what is conscious and unconscious, as well as become infallible

Vera: Why?

Frank: Because if we don't, then language as it relates to ideas and meaning will not be able to exclude what is subjective.

Vera: Is inductive generalization "psychologstic"?

Frank: All generalization is mental and hence psychological.

Vera: Do you accept inductive generalization?

Frank: It can suggest something original, but needs extensive evidence, qualification, or both to be reliable.

Vera: But don't politicians often give particular examples to help prove a general conclusion?

Frank: Yes, and it can be called "the politicians fallacy" since for inference about what is general to be valid it must accurately represent a general situation, and inference about special cases cannot directly range that far in practice, though one could make a more risky second inference from that.

Vera: Are universals real?

Frank: Not if everything real can change.

Vera: Which suggests there are no universals.

Frank: Bacon, and Locke rejected Scholasticism by rejecting universals and fake objectivity.

Vera: Is all fake objectivity subjective?

Frank: Yes, in so far as it is real at all, that is, with a capacity to influence or be influenced, but subjectivity as including what is mental or conscious should be sharply distinguished from subjective as what in fact has been affected by what is emotional or prejudicial.

Vera: Because it is possible to be relatively objective while being subjective in the first sense but not in the second?

Frank: Yes, since it is possible to be vulnerable to influence by what is emotional or prejudicial without actually being influenced by them in fact.

Vera: What do *you* mean by language?

Frank: In one sense, a totality of potential and actual expression used by a community of people which suggests one or more particular ideas or meaning to them but only with difficulty, incompletely, or not at all to outsiders. In another sense, it is an aspect of human understanding and hence is mental and subjective, but it can be hard not to objectify some aspects of it.

Vera: What do you mean by objective?

Frank: In a relative or absolute sense?

Vera: Both.

Frank: Relative objectivity can mean what we mentioned above being subjective in a good sense, free from emotion and prejudice. Or in a related sense or use being comparatively free from emotion and prejudice.

Vera: And absolute objectivity?

Frank: What is physically real but can never be made conscious. But "absolute" does not mean absolute certainty here, but what exists independently of both potential and actual human awareness.

Vera: Why is freedom from consciousness so important?

Frank: Because if nature is not free from it, then there would be no physical world. Everything would be mental and subjective.

Vera: But if everything physical is trans-conscious in a permanent or necessary way . . .

Frank: we can still refer to it by *intent* which by using inference and measurement can allow us to understand the external physical world which physical science has partly done, even if all thinking is literally mental and many parts often conscious.

In short, we have to use what is mental, such as reference, philosophy, and science to help us understand what is physical.

Vera: But what if there is only one type of reality?

Frank: We can still distinguish between what can be made conscious to us and what not, and we will probably still call what can be made conscious "mental" and what not "physical", even if in some ultimate sense they are one or of one general type.

Vera: What about God?

Frank: I hope God and Providence exist, but I am not sure how probable such things are.

Vera: Then you don't believe?

Frank: If to believe means to have faith, and faith means loyalty to hope or to what is good, then I do believe.

Vera: And epistemology?

Frank: I don't accept it in the sense of unconditional immediacy or unconditional certainty, but I call distinguishing between what can be made conscious and what cannot, to be the heart of epistemology.

Vera: Why isn't science considered foundation theory?

Frank: Because science rests on philosophical assumptions from semantics, epistemology, ontology, and value theory.

Vera: Do most scientists accept that?

Frank: When more of them recognize that learning is not understanding and training is not education, many of them probably will. But foundation theory does need improvement.

`Vera: Could that not come from a better understanding of
semantics, especially about meaning as intent and much more
vigorous rejection of rhetoric?

Frank: I would like to work harder toward that goal.

Vera: But so many other preliminary steps are needed.

Frank: Perhaps the first and most difficult one is to suggest to
students of abstract understanding that there are times when it
may be wiser to identify causes less with scientific laws and
more with the ability of particular human beings and processes
in nature to help influence other people and both the physical
world around us and the particular workings of our mind or
brain.

Vera: This may force you to defend more strongly practical
reason such as inductive logic, means-end logic, and cause-and-
effect logic, even if ideally one may prefer pure reason.

Frank: But only if they are ethical and properly qualified.

Vera: Nevertheless, if nothing can be proved to be
unconditionally certain, even in idealized logic, science, and
philosophy, then the apparent probability that practical reason
may not be unconditionally certain either, should not always or
necessarily be seen as a defect but as a challenge or fact of life.

Frank: Especially since neither idealized nor non-idealized
science seems, because of probable human limitations and
fallibility, to be able to be more than comparatively or
conditionally certain, such that some people may doubt if our
ideas can ever be true in more than a highly probable sense.

Chapter Two

PHILOSOPHY

Vera: What is your basic philosophy?

Frank: Do you remember the reply of Socrates to the Oracle of Delphi?

Vera: I think so. The Priestess was asked who was the wisest man in Hellas and she answered "Socrates", who replied when told: "I only know that I know nothing".

Frank: But he was not just being modest or a fallibilist; nor was he rejecting truth. He was merely arguing that there were always conditions to our understanding. For example, to see well we need light and good eyes. And to reason well we need the kind of logic best suited to solving the problem at hand. Many things are probably true or real, but dependent or conditional, as is our understanding of them.

Vera: So he was largely rejecting unconditional certainty about them?

Frank: As I understand it, assuming Plato had the story right.

Vera: So your philosophy is conditional and fallible.

Frank: I am a conditional probabilist, at least such is an underlying assumption, yes.

Yes: And your epistemology, ontology, and value theory?

Frank: To give short answers: Positions presupposed by heliocentrism, atomism, representative perception, and hope.

Vera: Which book changed your philosophy the most?

Frank: While I have learned that it can be hard to overcome initial views in semantics and philosophy, some books have made a big difference, specially accidental reading of a work by Hans Vaihinger called *The Philosophy of As if*.

Vera: What did it alter?

Frank: He didn't alter my position so much as complete it. I feared that my version of probabilism lacked an amendment allowing for quick and decisive action. His approach provided the answer by allowing me to act *as if* I were certain when I was not, provided that I honestly admitted the gap between probabilism in thought and occasional certaintism in action.

Vera: When did this "completion" take place?

Frank: Just before I entered graduate school in philosophy?

Vera: Oh dear. So you developed your own philosophy that early?

Frank: All my professors at Berkeley save one opposed conditional probabilism. Wittgenstein and Logical Positivism became their obsession at the time.

Vera: How did you survive?.

Frank: It was a fight all the way, given my views on semantics. I was courteous and qualified myself, but it wasn't sufficient.

Vera: Expressing qualification can be risky, and means weakness in war.

Frank: No. Intending qualifiation is good, and one should express it *often enough* to seem as reasonable and undogmatic as possible, and this also applies to you, young lady.

Vera: Many thinkers qualify claims through fear of being criticized, but you held them as a matter of principle.

Frank: Yes, I began to think that while theoretical truth meant correspondence with reality that practical truth was in the qualification.

Vera: But which one do you really prefer, dear master?

Frank: Both theories involve correspondence, one with reality and one with weight of supporting evidence, and when degree of belief matches that weight, then "truth is in the qualification".

Vera: What kind of qualification?

Frank: That which reduces the pretentiousness of claims about truth and reality down to the actual weight of evidence in so far as we understand it . . .

Vera: so that we do not believe more strongly than the weight of evidence justifies?

Frank: Correct.

Vera: But again, what are the different kinds of qualification?

Frank: There are many. Some are factual or refer to exceptions, Some are linguistic, stylistic, or logical to make something seem more understandable or plausible, and most reduce the degree or extent of a claim that something is true, real, or right.

Vera: But more certainty about less, merely protects us from criticism. It doesn't clarify truth as correspondence with unreduced, unqualified existence.

Frank: Most qualification reduces the degree or extent of correspondence to make our claim more likely to be true to the existing weight of evidence.

Vera: I want to know unvarnished, absolute truth!

Frank: We all do, hence we carry out more research so that our claims come closer to absolute truth while also matching weight of evidence.

Vera: Is your view a revival of a theory of double truth? Such as Averroes the Moslem scholar is said to have advocated?

Frank: No, just common sense and non-idealized science.

Vera: Or like Bacon when he warred against rhetoric as both Idols and bad style? As if there were two kinds of truth about rhetoric?

Frank: If there were only one use of the word, then one might blame him for holding different theories of truth, but rhetoric as mere stylistic beauty or fine embellishment is very different from trying to persuade without accompanying evidence.

Very: But cannot beauty and style enhance influence?

Frank: Yes, and Bacon did that with his *Essays*, but with accompanying evidence. I must also remark that you have clearly read history of philosophy and also thought about it.

Vera: But is Bacon still useful three centuries later?

Frank: He supported common sense and experimentation, and even caught a cold carrying one out, and died from it.

Vera: Yes, yes. I remember. He left his carriage, packed a dead chicken with snow to see if it would help preserve the meat.

Everyone remembers that story. But I fear it has become trite and hackneyed.

Frank: But its still true and still important.

Vera: If clichés are important.

Frank: You should judge non-fiction by its truth, value, and what one can learn from it, not style, originality, or feeling.

Vera: Excessive repetition of familiar proverbs and old stories can . . .

Frank: reveal how hard it is for some people to infer what is fresh or important after seeing snow and chickens for a hundred times, but Bacon did it, loved proverbs, and so can you.

Vera: On the other hand, hearing or reading the same thing too many times can weaken our appreciation of its importance.

Frank: If we let such things influence our judgment. First, if we are willing to take the time to find a wise proverb we can, like: "Action speaks louder than words". And second, Bacon probably heard from farmers that snow and ice might help preserve meat, so as a good scientist he decided one day to get out of his carriage to test that theory. Yes, snow can be boring after a while, and he had often written about science, but this time it woke the real scientist in him. This made the story important.

Vera: If he hadn't died from it, then it probably would have been forgotten.

Frank; I apologize, I shouldn't have gotten angry. But it is wrong to apply literary or emotional criteria to non-fiction, or even fiction if our main goal is to learn and not just to feel. New impressions can matter, but truth almost always matters more.

Vera: I am sorry for seeming prejudiced like many literary critics who let emotion influence judgment instead of hard evidence, and I recognize that words like "trite", "cliché", and "hackneyed", were as bad as rhetoric and for the same reason: they constitute or encourage prejudgment.

 Frank: I'm sorry too. I am not really a chameleon for praising you one minute and finding fault the next.

Vera: They adjust by changing color, but truth is immortal.

Frank: If Caesar crossed the Rubicon, then it will always be true that he crossed it.

Vera: But if the weight of evidence changes?

Frank: Reality determines truth; weight of evidence probable truth, and man merely opinion about truth.

Vera: Is science mere opinion?

Frank: Non-idealized science can be literally true.

Vera: And idealized science counterfactually true?

Frank: If it doesn't correspond to the real world, yes.

Vera: I don't think most mathematical scientists want to hear that.

Frank: Many abstract thinkers continue to emphasize logical as formal reasoning after more practical people have switched to causal and historical thinking.

Vera: Is that why Bell argued that if mathematicians have not discovered anything great before the age of 25, then . . . ?

Frank: Bell was not really that dogmatic, but brilliance in one type of reasoning often discourages us from studying other kinds, which can seem less promising even if more practical.

Vera: Were you so weak at logic and mathematics as to welcome causal and historical thinking?

Frank: No, geographical and historical reading came first, which made it hard to consider abstract deduction as either sufficient or very enlightening.

Vera: Still, much qualification is often hard to distinguish from being evasive or afraid.

Frank: But it can be done. Part of the search for truth, which is part of common sense, is to avoid dogmatism and exaggeration, and qualification can help cure both. As for criticism, I agree with Popper that we should welcome it, since it gives us an opportunity to improve our beliefs and assumptions.

Vera: I didn't know you were Popperian.

Frank: Sir Karl Popper was a great philosopher, but I think he was wrong that meaning is objective and that all science is idealized. In those two respects he was no better than the Logical Positivists.

Which is worse? scepticism as under-belief or dogmatism as over-belief?

Frank: Over-belief, that is, going beyond the weight of evidence. Most under-belief is merely a type of caution; nor is it right to confuse scepticism with either probabilism or nihilism. If nothing is unconditionally certain, then a measure of doubt or scepticism is justified.

Vera: Since I agree, why hit a strawman?

Frank: Or straw woman?

Vera: I like to be flattered, but I'm not a horse.

Frank: Praise can be honest

Vera: From a man? Since when?

Frank: Let's get back to belief as a matter of degree.

Vera: As you suggest, it should vary with weight of evidence.

Frank; And if it doesn't?

Vera: It is irrational or irresponsible. But I suspect you are against belief in principle.

Frank Not at all, if degree of belief never goes beyond what the weight of evidence justifies. I also hope that many good things will become true in the future, even if they seem very improbable now.

Vera: Just as doubt can be doubted to infinity, so degrees of belief can be under-supported ad infinitum.

Frank: Rarely in a concrete or causal way. If I cannot believe that the future will always be good I can still hope that it will and remain loyal to that hope, which some people call "religious faith".

Vera: Mere hopers are atheists, for all that.

Frank: But belief in hope is religious.

Vera: I admit some religions are atheist like Buddhism.

Frank: Rational belief cannot go beyond the weight of evidence; yes, most Buddhists are non-theists and often more religious than Christians; and loyalty to hope, is an honest and rational type of religious faith.

Vera: I also like hope. But belief can make one feel better, even if it is actually over-belief.

Frank: In my opinion belief never made anything true, over-belief anything certain, and under-qualification anything rational or reasonable.

Vera: What is the difference?

Frank: Pure reason is rational, and practical reason is . . .

Vera: both rational *and* reasonable?

Frank: Yes. Only what is true and practical can be both.

Vera: Many people think they are one, and even you sometimes seem to assume that.

Frank: Many things are hard to distinguish, but if doing so is important we should try.

Vera: Biographers distinguish between real persons, and Scholastics between what is abstract.

Frank: Not always, but as a quasi-historian I do have trouble distinguishing between relative certainty and high probability.

Vera: As I have between certainty and necessity.

Frank: I think I may be able to distinguish conditional from unconditional necessity, and conceivably, even absolute from unconditional necessity, even if neither contrast is concrete or has real examples, but what would "relative necessity" mean?

Vera: Many things seem to be certain beyond a reasonable doubt, and shouldn't they deserve more than mere hope and potential belief?

Frank: Very probably, yes.

Vera: Like Descartes *Cogito*, even if it does rest on assumptions?

Frank: Yes, and I also admit that where action is concerned we should often act *as if* we were certain, provided that no one is misled about our position.

Vera: Even about fictional characters in dialogues?

Frank: I stand corrected.

Vera: I am tired of *expressing* both sceptical and factual qualification when more careful listeners already take both into account.

Frank: Everyone is not careful, perceptive, or fair. And if you were really against rhetoric you would not even want to hide qualification.

Vera: A dogmatic stance by seeming authoritative is indeed a kind of rhetorical trick which can persuade some people in the absence of supporting evidence, but that was not my intent.

Frank: To merely intend to act is not to act.

Vera: But to intend to mean is to mean?

Frank: Yes.

Vera: I think the situation is more complicated.

Frank: Perhaps, but it is natural to express less qualification the more emotional we become or the more important or heated a point or argument seems.

Vera: But if we were truly responsible, then the more important then the more careful we would be about making sure we add qualification in either intent, expression, or both.

Frank: It is neither healthy nor wise to consider everything important. It could strain the emotions. Humor and relaxation also matter.

Vera: Logicians will notice a flaw in your reasoning, since to matter is to be important, even if your intended point is sound. Everything is not important and should not be. On the other hand, I do think like most women that we generally consider more things to be important than most males.

Frank: Like domestic labor? Right, but intense concentration is different.

Vera: True. Women often lack the stamina and energy to concentrate as intently, which can partly explain why a few men seem very creative or profound.

Frank: All honest praise is welcome.

Vera: Even if false for most of your sex?

Frank: Even then

Vera: As a gesture of good will?

Frank: Yes.

Vera: I prefer the truth.

Frank: I suspect we may appear one-sided, since many important people saying important things disagree with both of us about many things, and honestly believe that language is truly objective and that all science is idealized.

Vera: But if we are right, then it is they who are one-sided.

Frank: Or more accurately. since all truth is selective, then we are properly one-sided and they are improperly so.

Vera: Or even more accurately, Real truth corresponds with what exists, and merely relative, objectified, idealized, and fake truth do not.

Frank: If idealization is necessary, then perhaps an amount of fake objectivity could be unavoidable if that kind of science and philosophy are to prosper. As an epistemological representist about perception, truth, and art, I can enjoy the appearance of objectivity in an aesthetic manner without having a bad conscience because what is probably or actually true, real, or right fails to be just as beautiful.

Vera: I smell more rhetoric.

Frank: Since we want to tell the truth and convey it to listeners and readers, then only what is likely to mislead or deceive should be criticized in that context as "rhetoric". Most common and even uncommon assumptions do not do that, especially if properly qualified in expression or cited using footnotes.

Vera: What seems most plausible is often most deceptive, precisely because it does seem so plausible.

Frank: If it leads to less examination and research, yes, but normally, the more plausible the more likely to be true.

Vera: To seem more plausible, even the mighty may cheat.

Frank: Just as all untruths are not lies, so everything clever is not cheating, There must be intended error to be immoral.

Vera: What about Kant who intended to misidentify Berkeley's idealism in order to suggest that he himself was a "realist"?

Frank: I don't believe it. Can you prove that?

Vera: I can try. I remember a few things about the history of philosophy. Young Berkeley called sensations "ideas" and he identified the external world with them, hence he became widely known as an idea-list. Kant, however, instead, identified Berkeley's supernatural world with ideal-ism, and since Kant did not think we could prove the existence of that world using science or philosophy this suggested to some of his less perceptive followers that his own philosophy being so different from Berkeleyan "ideal-ism" was a form of realism, even though on occasion honesty intervened and the great Königsberger sometimes admitted that he himself was an idea-list, but a "critical" one.

Frank: Every philosopher who does not want to have his own approach tarred by the bad connotation of a predecessor or earlier philosophy is likely to re-define words.

Vera: It is still rhetoric and still cheating.

Frank: You asked me to explain my approach to semantics, and I am trying, but students obsessed with their own ideas, and especially with dark innuendoes generally learn less.

Vera: Or have less to learn.

Frank: I thought you wanted to learn as much as possible.

Vera: I do.

Frank: And are not learning enough from me?

Vera: I am on your side. I favor the obvious semantic and practical truth that people mean and not words, sentences, and propositions. And by using that truth it is easier to discover the difference between honest reasoning and rhetoric.

Frank: I suppose you are anxious to learn more than I can deliver, but sometimes it is better to reflect. Most academics in their capacity as both authors and audiences continue sticking with the notion that words, conventions, propositions, and definitions mean, and merely resort to "authors or people mean", if at all, when communication obviously fails, and in those exceptional cases when they actually want to understand what an author is driving at better. But bad intent is evil.

Vera: Good!

Frank: Also, the world is simply not made as if associations we add to words were determined by the words themselves. Nor do dictionaries and conventions tell us about value-connotation, which can prove that language is not always or even normally objective, and instead, it is noticed tone of voice or unnoticed prejudgment which can change, taint, or reverse meaning.

Vera: But shouldn't everyone want and try to understand and communicate better?

Frank: Perhaps in theory, but inconsistently in practice.

Vera: But why not if the search for truth comes first and learning from intent-focused semanticists can be a major way of coming closer to the truth?

Frank: Remaining with the illusion that words mean has become so ingrained in dictionaries and common usage over the last millennium that even occasional audience focus on to mean as to intend in order to help us communicate better is still not generally acknowledged as more fundamental.

Vera: But academics concerned with better communication as a path to better understanding of truth and reality should know better than to suppose that impotent words can do something in a potent way, especially something as active as to help cause something to mean. If the notion that words mean has lasted for a millennium or longer, then giving priority to the fact that people actually mean may need an intellectual revolution to prevail. I am ready! To the barricades!

Frank: Most semanticists have known the truth for a long time, but we are not strong enough to overcome such a deeply entrenched contrary view, unless we use rhetoric, which we despise. But if this book can generate support, then gradual persuasion could well "pick up steam".

Vera: But in a rational world truth *has* to prevail.

Frank: I wish you were older and more familiar with how academic fashion-chasing and the worship of current authority can combine to keep back much genuine advance.

Vera: I don't want to assimilate with such people if it means to abandon the fight for truth, especially in semantics and science.

Frank: Why do you think this dialogue is being presented? To abandon the fight for truth?

Vera: No, but you should be shouting "People mean" from the roof tops!

Frank: I strongly favor *authors* associating normal signification with words *as if* words could mean or have meaning

Vera: Even if meaning as intent is more basic?.

Frank: Yes, if causation as *influence* is really primary, but I also think that *audiences* should try as hard and fairly as they can to master what authors most likely intend and assume.

Vera: You don't need italics for emphasis in spoken dialogue.

Frank: Sorry! You may have missed my point again?

Vera: What point?

Frank; It may come as a shock, my dear born-yesterday, but many if not most academics and scientists identify causes with relations and laws and *not* with agents or forces as influence. For them, what is passive in terms of causal influence can still help cause in terms of laws or necessary relations. In their eyes, scientific laws have replaced "historical influence", and for others it is mathematical functions that have done it. Indeed, some philosophers want to replace space and time themselves as if only formal relations exist.

Vera: But if such extreme views are literally false or an exaggeration, then how could such an approach be either scientific or practical?

Frank: Many philosophers and scientists welcome idealization as much as we criticize it. Reduction and simplification are often treated as virtues, more so than the time-consuming research of we historians who want to be detailed, accurate, and understand as much as possible about non-idealized truth and non-idealized reality in a non-idealized way.

Vera: I agree that presentist "matter" is mental, and that real physical particulars are consciously indirect and causal, and contain too many variables to have all parts and aspects deducible from laws or claims about them, since the particulars are more complex than the laws.

Frank: I apologize. You are not an immature know-it-all, but an ambitious young lady with a good mind. In fact, you are learning fast and becoming more astute, but perhaps somewhat prematurely.

Vera: I appreciate forgiving "youthful haste", but how can learning be premature?

Frank: Studying semantics without knowing its history can be premature.

Vera: How?

Frank: By using current ideas to misunderstand or prejudge older ones.

Vera: You haven't even told me how you learned semantics.

Frank: Its not very interesting.

Vera: But you wrote a book on it, didn't you?

Frank: A manuscript, Yes.

Vera: Please. Let me read it.

Frank: It was too emotional to publish.

Vera: You identify meaning with intent, but won't even describe your own intentions.

Frank: That was my first book manuscript. I wrote it while still a student.

Vera: There is mystery here.

Frank: Lets drop it. I want to seem fair and objective.

Vera: Then I will start by reading the history of semantics.

Frank: I'm not aware of a book yet which describes what really happened.

Vera: The "good guys" lost?

Frank: Yes.

Vera: And it still hurts?

Frank: Yes.

Vera: Okay, I'll let you go now, but one day . . .

Frank: Please change the subject.

Vera: So I'll have to reconstruct the real history.

Frank: You are also becoming a philosopher, and fortunately with a thick skin and a tendency to forgive and forget my many faults.

Vera: Have you also forgiven your teachers from fifty years ago?

Frank: I would if I could.

Vera: Or could if you would?

Frank: I promise to try again.

Vera: If semantics has ethical roots, have you evolved to the point of wanting to forgive and forget?

Frank: Yes.

Vera: But can you actually do it?

Frank: I have not always succeeded in the past.

Vera: What about science?.

Frank: It is my turn to ask you questions. Do you think social skill is more important for scientists than to make great discoveries ?

Vera: No.

Frank: That writing style is more important than content?

Vera: No.

Frank: That scientific consensus determines truth?

Vera: No.

Frank: Or that it is more scientific to seem objective than to be objective?

Vera: No.

Frank: Or that it is more scientific to footnote authors by initials like R. Brown, H. Jones, and W. Smith so that they can be easily confused with other R, Browns, H. Jones, and W. Smiths?

Vera: Of course not. That sounds like a rhetorical question, even if real objections to them normally have little to do with rhetoric or "disguised statements", and almost everything to do with the difficulty in answering them without agreeing with the person who asks the question. Far from not being interrogative, they are often the most challenging questions of all.

Frank: But they do raise the issue of author intent in a very major way.

Vera: Yes, but I also think we have to honestly admit how very difficult it can be to accurately determine what the main or relevant intentions and assumptions of other people are, and sometimes even our own.

Frank: I remember an unusual tale about what some people would call a rhetorical question. The story was that when an Italian follower asked Napoleon when he escaped from Elba with less than 2, 000 men whether in addition to liberating France he also intended to liberate Italy. Bony replied as a Corsican from an island long under Genoese and hence under Italian influence before it was sold to France: "Am I not Italian?" which of course while perhaps pleasing his interlocutor with what might have seemed like a positive answer, actually left the question open, since it was clearly far too early for him to decide what to do about Italy with such a miniscule army.

Vera: Your account is a good example of what I mean. Bonaparte was obviously not making a statement. It was a real question for which he himself clearly had no answer, even if he was willing to mislead the Italian as if he did have one.

Frank; Granted. Trying to fathom human intent is often little more than guessing in the absence of more information, while casting aspersions or insufficiently supported criticism can seem unethical as well as dangerous for one's own reputation as a historian or researcher. Most academic fields and sciences are also social communities where it can normally seem wiser *not* to understand all that other people intend, assume, want to communicate, or are driving at, as if scholars and scientists need only be concerned with their own work and not with that of others or their likely motivations, or how other mental or physical factors may have influenced them. Human laws when applied and the military can also demand obedience rather than "backtalk". In short, the probable reality of causes as influence need not and socially speaking probably should not be directed too often at the thinking and actions of our immediate colleagues and especially not our legal superiors. But of course a world-figure like Napoleon was and is still fair game for opinions, both speculative and scientific.

Vera: If what is merely apparent is mental like an image or sensation, then the phrase "apparent objectivity" sounds odd, but perhaps merely because we are defining "apparent" in two different ways, and because we think that only what is physical and hence trans-conscious can be fully objective.

Frank: Such reflections are both semantically and philosophically important, but if a major purpose of social behavior is to stay out of trouble with one's colleagues, then either one must avoid being trapped in academic departments altogether or at least be extraordinarily careful or silent. Journal debates still seem possible, but to raise dust by saying what one thinks within a single department is surely asking for expulsion or removal. *Harmonia mundi.*

Vera: Still, some deep researchers usually put intellectual above social concerns.

Frank: Alone at one's computor, perhaps, but elsewhere, it can be too risky if the academic world matters, except with a very few close intellectual supporters or no one at all. Honesty is not always a social virtue, especially if it suggests a measure of dishonesty in the intentions and assumptions of colleagues. Is seeming, or pardon the expression, appearing objective always enough to avoid criticism?

Vera: I'm willing to speak openly about semantics and philosophy with anyone and everyone.

Frank: But are you willing to pay the price?

Vera: What price?

Frank: Having to change professors, departments, universities, and spending fifteen years as a graduate student.

Frank: You seem to advise that students with a unique philosophy of their own on entering graduate school act as cautiously as if they lived in a hostile dictatorship.

Frank: I was not prepared for almost total opposition, and like you I was open and argumentative. We are lucky to find each other.

Vera: And like you, I fight back, and still have to keep changing professors.

Frank: To change the subject, perhaps it is time to distinguish again between relative and absolute objectivity . . .

Vera: which few people define in the same way?

Frank: I do not want to sound harsh, but it is not always necessary to finish my sentences for me.

Vera: Where did you study philosophy?

Frank: As a graduate student?

Vera: Yes.

Frank: Mostly UC Berkeley and UCLA.

Vera: When?

Frank: Off and on during the fifties and sixties while normally supporting oneself with part-time jobs.

Vera: Why did you switch to history?

Frank: Because Wittgenstein and Carnap were in fashion, and were the type of presentists who had almost no understanding of indirect philosophy or representism, not to mention mind-matter dualism and conditional probabilism.

Vera: And their semantics objectified language and meaning?

Frank: Yes, but let us get back to philosophy and away from hostile philosophers and what they did in those days. How can I appear even relatively fair and relatively objective, when you keep digging into painful battles from long ago?

Vera: You never gave up.

Frank: But linguistically objectified presentism still matters in the social, philosophical, and book world.

Vera: I feel confused. If matter is trans-conscious and mind can be made conscious at least in principle, then how can what is physical be a "surface phenomenon" and intent and assumption normally something hidden from our own awareness?

Frank: Because we have an intention to do something does not always mean that it is currently conscious to us or even that it ever was fully conscious. As for "surface phenomena", that is an expression which is not always literally intended. Furthermore, consciousness and intent at least appear to be different types of mental existence and we often follow what we intend to do without always being conscious of the intention.

Vera: I guess I should have realized that myself. Part of wisdom should be to know when something is to be taken literally and when figuratively.

Frank: Machine communication, for example, may exist between robots and other machines, but while some aspects of human transfer of information may be physical and seem able to be interpreted literally, wisdom can require that we make a lot of distinctions which rarely occur to us. For example, while everything literally physical is objective, these two words normally mean different things in terms of the notion that words can mean or have meaning, the normal meanings are not interchangeable.

Vera: I know that, do not interchange them, and probably should resent being talked down to. Nor am I fully happy that you seem to be regressing back toward talking about alleged word-meaning instead of discussing person-meaning, which is the heart of your intent-based theory of semantics and now largely mine.

Frank: I'm sorry if anything I said implied disrespect, I do have the impression which I hope is not so unalterable as to be a prejudice that one's age can make a difference in depth of understanding. Yes, I believe that human communication has mental and physical aspects, and while I do indeed reject the notion that words literally mean, that view is still so widespread and become a matter of habit with most people that even I often use it, even if I know better.

Vera: There are indeed different habits of association, but habits can almost always be broken and frequently are, and as you yourself keep emphasizing there is no necessary relation between words and meaning or expression and meaning.

Frank: Or between what is physical and objective, even if everything physical is objective and nothing mental is objective, at least not in a strict sense. Nor does this imply that I am opposed to relative objectivity which I support about both mind and matter and hence about what is trans-conscious in principle.

Vera: Would it help to improve dictionaries?

Frank: Yes, and with the mental associations or connotations we make with actual spoken and written words noted there. The editors of dictionaries try to do their best, but ignore a lot that is part of meaning or can influence it, such as mental rhythm, tone of voice, and the value-connotation of words.

Vera: So dictionaries are partly to blame for miscommunication and the explosion of rhetoric in politics and the social sciences and implosion of most bookstore interest in physical science when expressed in objectified and hence Neo-Scholastic terms.

Frank: Not exactly. Dictionaries even though physical themselves can still be helpful about normal meaning as signification, spelling, parts of speech, syllable recognition, and synonyms, but for what particular persons actually intend at particular places and times or if other people have different intentions and assumptions than our own, then as you say, maximum communication can require inquiry into what is mental and subjective while virtually all dictionaries still have a long way to go to be as helpful as they conceivably could be. Spoken language still remains much richer than written expression with dialogues attempting to help fill the semantic gap. On the other hand, there are some words which can be found in books but are rarely spoken, though one can argue that the reverse is more common, and which if used more often in writing could make communication easier between author and audience.

Vera: But isn't all inquiry literally mental and hence subjective?

Frank: We think so, but many mathematicians and logicians given to idealization often want to believe that inquiry can really be objective, and that what is called "objective appearance" is not just conscious appearance and hence subjective, but is objective fact, even if such a position may logically require belief in abstract universals or Popper's "World 3".

Vera: No one is perfect.

Frank: I apologize for letting myself be carried away.

Vera: Then please stop.

Frank: I'm finished.

Vera: What does connotation *really* mean?

Frank: Everything does not have either an intrinsic or secret meaning, but in causal terms the associations people make with words constitute connotation, except that a main or basic connotation is often called the denotation of the word in everyday life. Philosophers, as already mentioned following John Stuart Mill define "denotation" differently as if words could refer to things, which is also evidence that Mill, a presentist with a phenomenalist type of position, rejected causation as influence in a way which allowed him to still think that mere words or language could literally refer.

Vera: Why do so many philosophers and scientists hold so ferociously and tenaciously to what seems contrary to both common sense and semantic fact?

Frank: Because they hold different assumptions than most people about the external physical world, or even deny its existence or "knowability"; and also because they reject causation understood in terms of physical and mental influence, or they have been persuaded by certain philosophers, especially early in life or before they read books with a different point of view.

Vera: Were you influenced by certain philosophers early?

Frank: If so, I am not aware of it now, but I was when I later read Plato, Descartes, and Locke, but it was a popular book called *The Tyranny of Words* plus studying so much physiology and many optical illusions in a course in experimental psychology which probably made indirect realism and the representative theory of perception seem to be so obviously true when used to help understand the probable character and existence of the external physical world.

 Vera: Were you ever attracted by the image or mirage that language and meaning are objective and that language and mathematics can literally determine meaning?

Frank: I liked mathematics, but I preferred concrete causes to abstract ones. But I must admit that I was thirty years old before I fully realized that many academics really do identify causes with laws and not with particular causal agents or forces, or they think the laws can somehow influence or control them.

Vera: Why do you think they think like that?

Frank: I am not sure, but many people who like to generalize or idealize tend to imagine that laws as abstract patterns can somehow actually make things happen, especially if linked to their conception of religion. But I wonder if the assocation is really fixed or rigid, since Berkeley, for example, was presentist and theist, while Newton was representist but also theist, and among the non-theists Mach was presentist and Lenin was representist. One seems to find both the religious and non-religious on all sides of epistemological and ontological issues. Thus it can be hard to argue that one's religion or non-religion determines one's basic philosophy, though of course there are other aspects of philosophy besides epistemology and ontology and of religion outside of theism and non-theism.

Vera: Couldn't some academics use the notion that laws are causes to help justify that they are superior to ordinary people, especially the military and sports-minded who naturally often think of causes in terms of force or influence?

Frank: To be fair, many people, academic and not, who consider themselves weak or who rightly oppose bullies, whether individual, national, or international, may well favor causes as laws for what they regard as ethical reasons.

Vera: What do you think?

Frank: I think that scientific laws can help us understand how idealized types of things happen under idealized conditions, but as a biographer and historian, I also believe that the behavior of particular human beings at particular places and times is usually better understood in terms of causes as particular agents or influence, even if only a totality of relevant factors can fully determine anything. So I support appealing to both laws and influence, but with qualification and under different conditions.

Vera: Did you always reject Logical Positivism and its analytic continuation?

Frank: No, I liked their attitude toward science, but not what seemed to me to be their ruthless and unfair rejection of all other types of philosophy than their own.

Vera: But aren't we often told that analytic philosophy has corrected the sins of Logical Positivism?

Frank: But alas, they still objectify language and meaning, while still trying to exclude foundation theory by calling it "metaphysical".

Vera: And still attempt to replace meaning as intent and physical objects with "physical object language"?

Frank: Unlike leopards, they have changed some of their spots, but I was appalled by what seemed to be their ignorance of most earlier philosophy.

Vera: Were you upset by their rejection of indirect realism and mind-matter dualism, as "metaphysical or "meaningless?

Frank: I was more upset by their use of rhetoric and prejudgment in their system of classification, since they keep employing words there with strong value connotations against their critics and opponents.

Vera: Words like "metaphysical", "psychologistic", and meaningless"?

Frank: Yes.

Vera: And especially against you?

Frank: No. I was only a minnow, easily ignored.

Vera: But they made it hard to get a doctorate?

Frank: At both Berkeley and L.A. But here we go again. Please stop. I don't want to think about those days.

Vera: Do most scientists realize the extent to which positivist and analytic methodologists have tried to manipulate and change science?

Frank: No. Many scientists think they oppose positivism while actually assuming many of their presentist views.

Vera: Should we call positivists philosophers or mere methodologists?

Frank: They would like to appear to be harmless methodologists while still calling themselves philosophers, but since many have a deeper agenda and want to change science to better fit presentist and formal reduction, then one might better call them:

Vera: Would-be intellectual dictators?

Frank: Only in the sense of attempting to force many other philosophers and historians out of philosophy departments and weakening the interest of many scientists and the general public in philosophy. Most are intelligent, but not very knowledgeable about other fields or even the history of their own discipline. And many still objectify language and meaning in counterfactual ways.

Vera: But they reject indirect and causal realism . . .

Frank: in favor of "a physical object language"

Vera: Even if such rests on false semantics?

Frank: Yes, as if language and meaning were really objective.

Vera: But wouldn't it be wonderful if semantics, science, and philosophy all adopted *sound* foundation assumptions?

Frank: I am not sure what you mean. I remember three different approaches to what is allegedly certain. First, many traditional philosophers often thought that nothing could be more reliable than the assumptions on which science or religion are based. Second, logical empiricists almost all imagine that nothing is more certain than formal logic or sensory impressions. And third, many representists and physical scientists have come to believe that measurement by machines in the absence of interfering observers is most trustworthy and genuinely objective.

Vera: Which alternative among the three do you prefer?

Frank: I tend to qualify the alleged certainty of sensory impressions, since so much depends on fallible recognition and identification and the fact that such can be influenced by emotions, habits, and memory which can all prove misleading or unreliable.

Vera: You haven't answered my question.

Frank: I prefer fundamental assumptions in philosophy and machine measurement in science, but I worry about the nature of measurement if too much rests on the peculiar characteristics of light.

Vera: "If I understand correctly and have not deceived myself" those are expressions which I used to call "weasel words" . . .

Frank: But if they help us approach truth, then they are good..

Vera: Contrary to Berkeley, Hume, and Kant, but like you, Lovejoy, and Popper, I think there is a real physical world, but unlike most or all of the mental realm it cannot be made directly conscious to us, but with the aid of inference, measurement, and good judgment it seems we can accurately understand a lot beyond the mental and conscious world.

Frank: Furthermore, physical science largely depends on three basic theories: heliocentrism, the representative theory of perception (even if slightly modified in gestalt terms), and the existence of atoms and molecules, which all ultimately require machine measurement plus a consciously *indirect* theory. First, we cannot literally sense or directly notice the real orbits of planets around the sun, but by using the heliocentric theory we can understand *why* "wandering" appearances that geocentrists and presentists identify with real planets appear to reverse directions for a while.

Vera: What about epicycles, deferents, and equants?

Frank: They are idealized extensions which can be important in distinguishing Copernican from Ptolemaic and Aristotelian astronomy but they have nothing to do with the basic difference between geocentrism and heliocentrism which is about whether the planets revolve around the earth or the sun.

Vera: Oh.

Frank: Second, the existence of external physical objects which radiate or reflect light into our eyes mean according to the representative theory of perception that the image in our head cannot be the same as the external objects which helps cause that effect.

Vera: This should be obvious.

Frank: And third, the atomic bomb rather forcefully demonstrated that atoms exist and have energy, and the inability to directly observe them without the help of enhancing machines proves that like matter itself their existence is actually trans-sensory and trans-conscious, that is, when we assume the truth of an amended version of the representative theory of perception as we should in terms of our best understanding, even if in much everyday life we simplify things *as if* matter could be directly noticed.

Vera: I agree with you scientifically and philosophically, but fear that too many people are too inattentive or lazy to switch from presentism to representism about matter.

Frank: It is the fact that matter as represented has more physical influence than it would have as merely presented to consciousness which makes it more practical in a causal sense.

Vera: And if merely "a physical object language"?

Frank: Then it would have little or no causal influence at all.

Vera: Then how can that old positivist theory survive?

Frank: It doesn't, except for people who identify causes with scientific laws or mathematical functions.

Vera: Including social theorists?

Frank: I am not sure there are any scientific laws outside of chemistry, physics, and astronomy.

Vera: Why not?

Frank: Because physical laws about types of things only seem able to fully apply when matter is so small or so distant that one can generalize as if the individual differences within types of particles, waves, or fields are too small to measure.

Vera: Is sociology which also generalizes or relies on mere statistics about little-known or unknown particulars within types reliable enough to be a science?

Frank: It is a field which changes so much from decade to decade to fit the latest academic fashions that one tends to question whether it even has a coherent foundation. Nevertheless, we both may undervalue the importance of social factors.

Vera: With all due respect, I will continue to "undervalue" social theorists, especially when they presume to challenge or consider themselves more important than much more reliable physical sciences. Sociologists also use vague terminology, do so little deep or exhaustive research, and use generalization and rhetoric to write false things about current and past history.

Many sociologists are little more than social activists and fashion-chasers.

Frank: I think you push matters too far. Sociology is a relatively new field and has not yet discovered enough reliable ways to understand and measure particulars as particulars, since it is hard to research and write enough reliable biographies about each person within the group it wants to generalize about.

Vera: No. Social generalities are as old as Protagoras and they don't seem to be getting much more reliable two thousand years later. They love generalities so much, that detailed biographies are the last thing they want to research, read, write, or use.

Frank: Few sociologists are full-fledged sophists like Gorgias and Protagoras. It is important to know something about social groups, classes, and conventions, even if is always risky to generalize when one doesn't know enough about all or even most of the particular individual persons included.

Vera: Should we oppose all generalization?

Frank: Much as generalizing seems to go beyond the weight of evidence as encouraged by believers in scientific laws, it would probably be impossible and almost certainly unreasonable to attempt to reject the whole thing, especially since we would need some measure of general truth even to think accurately on or express that rejection. But we can qualify generalizing as a process, as a form of understanding, and in expression by both intent and deed.

Vera: What different kinds of generalization exist?

Frank: Unqualified or insufficiently qualified *historical generalizations* can often be refuted by exceptions, but many *social generalizations*, whether qualified or not, are expressed or even intended in such a vague or holistic way as to be unclear, and while many people act as if unclarity refuted an argument, this is not literally so. We cannot properly refute what we do not reasonably-well understand, though curiously we must be able to understand enough of what we do not fully understand in order to correctly identify it as something we do not fully understand. *Idealized generalizations* as in physical science such as equations and laws are normally considered to be approximately true, even if they are counterfactual or could be refuted if enough relevant but excluded incompatible factors were influential enough in particular situations. *Philosophical generalizations* are a special type altogether and are rarely refuted by exceptions. They depend heavily on definition and semantics which is partly why we need these dialogues.

Vera: May I say something?

Frank: Like historical generalizations, the philosophical kind are normally about the real world, and if true they normally have universal application, but unlike traditional universals they can and should be qualified. But like social generalities they are often hard to understand in a clear or detailed way.

Vera: Please let me speak!

Frank: Later. What is somewhat unique about philosophical generalizations apart from the fact that all philosophy is general is that they are heavily dependent on specific definitions and specific underlying assumptions. Change the basic definitions and underlying assumptions and the philosophy is different. Furthermore, many philosophers try to prove their case more by logic and arguments than by evidence, since in a way they have none, at least to the extent as foundation theory that they are logically prior to empirical and experimental science. Thus to refute a particular philosophy one needs to start with more assumptions as prior thinkers held them. Refuting strawmen in philosophy probably exceeds all other fields.

Vera: I'm going to refute you with this linen gag.

Frank: Please wait! Only ten seconds more. Each movement and school of philosophical thought normally likes to believe that they have risen above their competition past and present while they themselves have kept correcting and refining details to better represent the philosophy of the future. Historians may enjoy describing how past hopes of this kind have almost always been dashed and replaced by very different philosophies using very different definitions and assumptions, like happened when Berkeley, Hume, and Kant attacked many of the assumptions of Bacon, Descartes, and Locke, who obviously never even suspected that attacks could come from such impractical angles as presentist reduction or Kantian "antinomies". Or put another way, few philosophies have ever seemed to accurately anticipate the perspective which would largely replace them, though in this example slipping from representism back to presentism in philosophy hardly mirrored progress in science, given the continuing representist aspects of heliocentrism, the representative theory of perception, and widespread acceptance of atoms and molecules. In short, there has been little cumulative development over the long run. One still needs to study philosophy from the Greeks to the present to become educated.

Vera: Are you finally finished, dear foghorn?

Frank: And in conclusion: failure to absorb past philosophy as a whole and lack of long continuity does not refute the importance of philosophy. All educated people have philosophical assumptions and as foundation theory it has to be understood in order to comprehend the deepest premises of all fields. Now what did you want to add?

Vera: Nothing.

Frank: What?

Vera: You talked so long, I forgot what I wanted to say, but it mattered to me more than most of your spiel.

Frank: I'm sorry. I couldn't stop.

Vera: And I can't start. Now I remember. While it could be wise to understand a vast range of different philosophies in order to finally help select what is best, first, it normally comes too late, since almost everyone has already adopted a position he finds hard to change, especially after having used initial belief to interpret subsequent reading and reflection, and second, recent philosophy and reinterpretation of old ideas can always add information and perspective to change what you call weight of evidence to prevent final judgment about what is best.

Frank: Nevertheless, I think that only a single philosophy can be fully true, and that serious philosophers should keep trying to understand and deepen their own assumptions without end.

Vera: How can one best define "epistemology" if you reject theory of knowledge?

Frank: As a conditional theory of reference and understanding.

Vera: Strictly speaking, an ontological contrast between existence and non-existence is enough to create a dualist position, since non-existence can always be given a positive name. Even atomism if contrasted with the void is really dualistic.

Frank: Nevertheless, one could still imagine a monism without even a fictional alternative to what exists, nothing to properly compare it with, and it has long been traditionally difficult to understand what is so inclusive that it cannot be compared, as if something were literally "incomparable".

Vera: Or make what is real in one sense unreal in another as could happen were one to try to treat both processes and unchanging universals as real, which might be confusing.

Frank: Some thinkers treat reference as if it could imply being or existence, but I think only what can exert influence is real.

Vera: If we refer to nothing as an absence of being, then if mere reference could make it something, then that would be even more confusing. Indeed, this kind of idealization reminds me of the Cretan and other so-called logical paradoxes which would cease to exist could one ever ask a real Cretan whether he meant to include himself as a liar at the time when he alleged that "All Cretans are liars."

Frank: Since you have clearly read Parmenides, then you already know that absence can always be defined as the presence of something else. If no paradoxes, then no idealization, and if no idealization then no science according to Popper. But I think he is mistaken that non-idealized understanding can never be scientific especially if the search for truth as correspondence with non-idealized reality is put first.

Chapter Three

RHETORIC

I
(SOCRATES)
PLATO

Belle: Please excuse me, Sir. Vera promised to come, but when she heard that you were simply going to practice a lecture, she thought I should come to help you.

Frank: How?

Belle: She said that sometimes you take too much for granted.

Frank: Oh, she did?

Belle: And that if I asked questions when I didn't understand what you were saying that it would help you.

Frank: And when you did understand?

Belle: I should just answer: "Yes", "I agree", or something like that.

Frank: Well, you can tell Vera . . .

Belle: I really do want to listen. I have taken courses in Ancient History and Ancient Philosophy.

Frank: Well . . .

Belle: I won't contradict you.

Frank: Actually, that could help.

Belle: Oh thank you for agreeing!

Frank: Its nothing. I mean good.

Belle; She said you often talked over the heads of your audience, and I will help a lot. I promise.

Frank: Are you ready, my dear?

Belle: Yes, completely!

Frank: And I thought a lecture was a monologue.

Belle: But dialogues are more interesting.

Frank: I must not let my normal philosophy, which is an attempt to use semantics to help bring history, science, religion, and common sense come closer together obscure the main focus of this lecture which is on several famous philosophers and scientists about how they employed value-connotation. The first thinker on our list is Socrates, who sometimes influenced the opinions of his students, not all of them, but particular ones including Plato and Xenophon who both wrote dialogues and reported on the trial of Socrates for having also influenced two other students, Alcibiades and Critias, for having respectively contributed to Athenian defeat against Sparta (404 B.C.) and having led an oligarchy of thirty tyrants after the fall of the city.

Belle: Why did the trial really take place?

Frank: I just said that, but if you want the legal or technical cause it was an old man who accused Socrates of corrupting the youth and introducing new gods into the city.

Belle: Thank you.

Frank: If we regard the trial of Socrates as about human influence or as possible proof of that influence, then it should follow that *particular persons, like Socrates, a user of words, could mean in the sense of intend assume, and refer.*

Belle: Obviously.

Frank: It was not "obvious". Many people think words mean and not people.

Belle: I'm sorry, but can't both be found in dictionaries?

Frank: Yes. Instead of acknowledging possible guilt for his influence on Alcibiades and Critias, which almost certainly would have helped his defence from a purely legal or court-perspective, in Plato's version Socrates refused to explicitly mention their names or deeds while praising himself for his loyalty to Athens, description perhaps seen as boasting, which apparently helped influence the jury against him. *His meaning was not objective or neutral*, but one-sided, *nor did language determine his meaning*, but very possibly an *intent* to influence the jury into both hearing his real opinion about himself and the trial and possibly to phrase his position so that in his old age he could die as a hero for philosophy and wisdom. In fact, he even refused to escape when given the chance, but drank the hemlock perhaps to seem victorious in death.

Belle: Are you sure?

Frank: It was a grand and memorable gesture and just as Marcus Portius Cato the younger committed suicide after reading Plato, first, to avoid Caesar the Dictator's proverbial mercy to fellow Romans, and second, to give a hero to the memory of the Roman Republic, so Socrates, by first, intentionally drawing the attention of the jury away from the purpose of the trial i.e. whether teachers might be partly responsible to a degree for the crimes of their students, and second, by avoiding the contrition and apology the jury wanted to hear, martyred himself, we presume, to put his vision of an Ideal society and ideal conception of human behavior above what would probably occur in the actual future in defeated Athens.

Belle: Good.

Frank: Since Socrates does not seem to have left any extant writings we will transfer our focus to Plato who did.

Belle: Have you read all his works?

Frank: Traditionally, the dialogues about the time between the trial of Socrates and those about the period up to his death are close to what Socrates actually thought and did, especially since Plato had been a young man in his twenties during that period and presumably knew many of the students of Socrates in person. On the other hand, because Plato's dialogue on the trial is not as historically informative in several ways as some of the dialogues of Xenophon it is natural for us to read them as well.

Belle: Wasn't he more of a historian than a philosopher?

Frank: Yes, but he had also been a student of Socrates and adds details Plato overlooked. Plato is perhaps best known for his *Republic* and it seems very probable that he emphasized his own ideas there and not those of Socrates. We will take a short critical sentence and then list the value-connotations which can be found there

2

Frank: Below is a long sentence from Book Ten of Plato's *Republic* starting with the tenth margin number which is 605, Jowett translation. The following short passages have been chosen by a method designed to randomize selection.

Belle: Why is "ten" significant?

Frank: I hope that if one can quote from the tenth chapter or tenth margin-number of famous books by famous philosophers that I can better identify which philosophers used value-connotation more than other philosophers. On the other hand, every book does not have ten chapters, some chapters are called "books", and all do not have margin-numbers, so that hard as we will try, we cannot always follow our plan in an exact way.

Belle: Even if they are not the most read chapters?

Frank: Right.

Belle: Do you think your method will work?

Frank: I don't know. Here is our first selection. It is by Plato, but probably comes closer to the views of Socrates.

> "Socrates: Then the imitative poet who aims at being popular is not by nature made, nor is his art intended to please or to affect the rational principle in the soul; but he will prefer the passionate and fitful temper, which is easily imitated.
>
> Glaucon: Clearly."

Frank: The list of words with bad connotations includes: *imitative, affect, fitful* and *not by nature made* plus words with good connotations like *rational* but intended here within a negative context and as if to be merely *popular* were bad, as if to *affect the rational principle* were bad, as if "the poet" being *passionate* were also bad here, and as if *to be easily imitated* were bad, but as if Glaucon's response, *clearly,* had a good connotation and reflected his approval of the sentence which Plato attributed to Socrates. Furthermore, it is only by presuming that we understand the intent attributed to Socrates that we can understand how terms which normally have good connotations by themselves can have bad associations in the actual context of this long and complex sentence, a kind which Jowett often seemed to consider appropriate.

Belle: So I'll be like Glaucon, a fifth wheel?

Frank: He served a purpose, and so will you.

Belle: Thanks. I'm trying.

Frank: Nor should we forget that many readers of Plato's works will sympathize with the apparent arguments of Socrates and that some of the words and phrases which have value connotations will be accepted by those readers, and at least in this context without inquiring into whether Greek poets were actually like they are described here and whether Plato is using rhetoric. Nor does Plato at least in this passage name a real poet so that actual evidence about him could be derived from other sources. Plato would clearly like to reach a general or universal conclusion about poets, but no amount of evidence is really very likely to prove such things. There will always be exceptions, and perhaps they will be a majority.

Belle: So Socrates was not always fair?

Frank: He tried to persuade.

Belle: By using rhetoric?

Frank: Yes, with the help of reasons.

Belle: But not strong enough to be evidence?

Frank: He was trying to generalize about most or all poets.

Belle: Or at least who memorize for the public.

Frank: But underqualified induction . . .

Belle: Was not the answer?

Frank: It rarely is.

3

ARISTOTLE

Frank: Let us consider Plato's student next, but unlike our short section on Plato it will have to be carried out in a somewhat more extensive way because he himself has written at more length and systematically on rhetoric and in a manner which is often considered to be authoritative. He generally favored good rhetoric and opposed bad rhetoric. And like almost everyone he was also sometimes guilty of using rhetoric unfairly.

Belle: If rhetoric makes speech sound better, then it may be easier to enjoy.

Frank: Aristotle preferred truth to enjoyment.

Belle: I like both.

Frank: The Stagirite, as Aristotle is often called because he came from the small Greek city of Stagira on the Macedonian border, apparently believed by his formulation of logic and much science that it was possible for many things to be true "beyond a reasonable doubt", even if such conditional certainty did not "logically" imply unconditional certainty. Contrary to Socrates and Arcesilaus as conditional probabilists, Aristotle would eventually win a reputation as "the master of those who know" as if there were no significant differences between certainty and *unconditional* certainty. We begin with six short quotations from the first pages of his book on rhetoric which seem reasonable and three more which we think are weak, or objectionable, and where we will describe and explain why we think so.

97

Some of Aristotle's Guidelines

1. Rhetoric may be defined as the faculty of observing in any given case the available means of persuasion.

2. It is clear, then, that rhetorical study, in its strict sense is concerned with the modes of persuasion.

3. Of the modes of persuasion furnished by the spoken word there are three kinds. The first depends on the personal character of the speaker; the second on putting the audience into a certain frame of mind; the third on the proof or apparent proof provided by the words of the speech itself.

4. Rhetoric is not bound up with a single class of subjects, but is as universal as dialectic.

5. Argument based on knowledge implies instruction, and there are people whom one cannot instruct. Thus we should use, as our modes of persuasion and argument, notions possessed by everybody . . . when dealing with the way to handle a popular audience.

6. The man who makes a good guess at the truth is likely to make a good guess at probabilities.

Three Difficult Ones

7. With regard to the persuasion achieved by proof or apparent proof: just as in dialectic there is induction on the one hand and syllogism or apparent syllogism on the other, so it is in rhetoric. The example is an induction, the Enthymeme is a syllogism, and the apparent Enthymeme is an apparent syllogism. I call the Enthymeme a rhetorical syllogism, and the example a rhetorical induc-

tion. Everyone who effects persuasion through proof does in fact use either Enthymemes or examples. There is no other way.

8. Suppose it were said, "The fact that Socrates was wise and just is a sign that the wise are just." Here we certainly have a sign, but even though the proposition is true, the argument is refutable, since it does not form a syllogism.

9. What is the nature of probability, of a sign, and of a complete proof, and what are the differences between them?

Belle: Aristotle is hard. Each word matters.

Frank: Unexpressed qualification is most to blame. Nor do I believe that propositions or syllogisms either carry or determine truth, since if meaning is in the intent and not in expression, form, or language, then it is the idea meant that is true or false, that is, corresponds with reality. Furthermore, if premises are false, and meaning is unclear or insufficiently qualified, then even syllogisms fall short of being unconditionally certain.

Belle: Is *your* language fully qualified?

Frank: No, but by intent my ideas and assumptions are. Aristotle's language and grammar-based approach rather notoriously led to Scholasticism during the Middle Ages because of the emphasis on language, logic, form, types, and the absence of enough research and reasonable assumptions and premises. Many modern philosophers of science seem to think that all that was lacking was empirical verification and falsification, that is, on the assumption that idealized, mathematical law-based science about idealized types of things under idealized conditions is the only kind of science, as young Carnap and old Popper appeared to hold.

Belle: I don't think many current philosophers agree with your doubts about idealized science.

Frank: If they did, there would be no point in writing.

Belle: But flat opposition rarely persuades.

Frank: Weight of evidence will normally do so, long after pre-judgment dies.

Belle: Then why worry about current opposition?.

Frank: That's a good point.

Belle: Or keep attacking scholastics?

Frank: Because it is a shame that they should return to prominence in science after Bacon and his Idols banished them

Belle: Don't we need formal logic?

Frank: Not very often. I prefer natural logic based on meaning as the intent and assumptions of real speakers under real conditions.

Belle: Modern science demands more.

Frank: Well they won't get it from me. I don't like to put words in other people's mouths. We should respect what other people intend instead of using formal logic to refute straw men.

Belle: If you were really neutral about prejudice and value-connotation, then you would stop trying to identify modern science and philosophy with scholasticism.

Frank: I just want to tell the truth to the best of my current understanding, and the truth appears to be that the word "scholastic" has a bad connotation for well-deserved reasons, mostly because it reminds us of excessive concern for school logic and objectified language unsupported by sound premises, new understanding, and weight of evidence. But I am happy to look for a less negative-sounding substitute like . . .

Belle: Please add fair words for the terms "school logic" and "objectified" as well.

Frank: Okay. "Form-based philosophy" for scholasticism; "university logic" for school logic, and "made-to-seem objective" for objectified, but initially other people may not know what I am referring to by the new words and phrases.

Belle: On reflection, please go back to your prejudicial words with the bad connotations, since they will reveal more quickly what a hypocrite you are in opposing rhetoric and value-connotation, when you so conspicuously use them yourself.

Frank: You still seem to think that language is objective and that words mean, but my alleged "hypocrisy", merely demonstrates how hard it is to avoid subjective language and value-connotation. Using the same methods we consider bad does not invalidate the criticism or always make us hypocritical.

Belle: I disagree. I think it does.

Frank: In criticizing something, if it really deserves criticism, and is a strong personal habit or very widespread, then it is very likely that we will sometimes fall into that bad conduct or attitude ourselves. Genuine hypocrisy must be deliberate. Otherwise it is merely inadvertent inconsistency of expression or thought which does not represent our best understanding.

Belle: One can always use that as an excuse.

Frank: I am not neutral in philosophy, and weight of evidence is not neutral either, but we can try to use it more to persuade in a legitimate manner, that is, which takes precedence over rhetoric value-connotation, and hasty judgment.

Belle: Mathematical scientists idealize without being scholastic or hypocritical, and using sound mathematical methods has added rigor and led to the greatest theoretical contributions to physics.

Frank: I am not sure that you understood what I said.

Belle: I understood what you did.

Frank: This is hopeless. Like most people, I think that the most important scientific *discoveries* are normally somewhat more important than the simplest and most abstract ways of formalizing them.

Belle: What discoveries?

Frank: That the earth and the other planets revolve around the sun and not around the earth, that atoms and molecules are real, even if they are too small to be noticed by our naked eyes, that sensory images are not external objects, and that most of them imperfectly represent a few aspects of real external objects, especially with respect to size, shape, and motion.

Belle: Those are merely philosophical discoveries rejected by most philosophers.

Frank: Is discovering that heliocentrism can explain the apparent retrograde motion of the planets which geocentrism cannot, philosophical or fact? Is discovering that electron microscopes can be used to identify molecules, and that we can now photograph many atoms, philosophical or fact? And is discovering that physical diseases like cancer can influence our bodies before we suffer pain as if the physical world were independent of consciousness, philosophical or fact?

Belle: They can all be explained differently.

Frank: In a way most reasonable non-philosophers can accept?

Belle: As a philosopher, I try to be consistent with the latest philosophy of science which rejects all metaphysics about the so-called physical world.

Frank: That view is closer to training and indoctrination than to education, which investigates many perspectives before . . .

Belle: losing its way into metaphysics?

Frank: How easily training becomes dogmatic and scholastic.

Belle: I prefer the latest science and latest philosophy to long refuted error. Please change the subject.

Frank: But I thought you like to study Greece and Rome?

Belle: Only to discover how we have improved upon both.

Frank: But have we in philosophy?

Belle: If not, then why do we teach the new stuff?

Frank: Perhaps from too little reading and too much prejudice.

Belle: I feel certain contemporary thought is better.

Frank: By using words like "certain" or "certainty" without expressed qualification, it can be hard to determine whether you mean conditional certainty, certainty beyond a reasonable doubt, or unconditional certainty.

Belle: Can't something simply be certain?

Frank: No. Lack of qualification increases ambiguity. Being highly probable may be relatively certain, or even certain "beyond a reasonable doubt", but it is still not *real* certainty because it is not *unconditionally* certain. Furthermore, if we are finite and fallible as all sane people think, then we are not unconditionally certain either, and should not simply claim to be certain or use the term without qualification, lest we confuse other people into thinking that we are unconditionally certain.

Belle: If we accept meaning as intent, as you propose, then when I say something is certain I mean more certain than your reply or prejudgment.

Frank: Then please only talk to people who accept your particular intent.

Belle: I'm talking to you, big shot, and I will say and mean whatever I want when I call something "certain".

Frank: Even if it misleads people?

Belle: Yes.

Frank: You can leave now!

Belle: What for?

Frank: Deliberate deception is unethical, and you just defended being unethical.

Belle: My truth is to stay happy, even if *you* think it is false, deceptive, or "merely relative".

Frank: You don't mean this.

Belle: I mean whatever I want to mean. I love fashion.

Frank: Fashion-chasing is rarely the surest road to truth.

Belle: Rational truth is irrational if it doesn't make me happy, and I enjoy being happy and laughing at old styles and fashions.

Frank: Philosophy is more than training and laughter at what is old.

Belle: Not for me.

Frank: Why do bright ladies bristle when I try to persuade them?

Belle: Because you are no good at it. Your rhetoric stinks.

Frank: I'm sorry, but I prefer to finish preparing my lecture without your assistance. I am becoming emotional and I want to become more reasonable and rational, and that is hard to do in your immediate presence. I wish you well, thank you for your questions and ideas, but the door is that way.

(Belle leaves.)

Frank: Now where was I? The last point may also help make clear that sceptics, probabilists, and certaintists are normally closer together in attitude and belief than they themselves often think. A man may think of himself as a sceptic because he rejects unconditional certainty, which almost everyone does, or a believer or dogmatist because he thinks he is certain about many things "beyond a reasonable doubt", but without being unconditionally certain. But to hide real doubts in order to persuade is hardly honorable, even if the doubts are minor or conditional. Thus, even most people who talk as if they were certain should admit that if they are not unconditionally certain, but only relatively certain because what the alleged certainty is about may only be highly probable, and not really true or real.

Frank: Below is a paragraph from Chapter Ten of Aristotle's *On Interpretation* from margin numbers 25 to 35 using the McKeon version of *The Basic Works of Aristotle*. (1941, 11th printing).

"It is evident, also that when the subject is individual, if a question is asked and the negative answer is the true one, a certain positive proposition is also true. Thus, if the question were asked 'Is Socrates wise?' and the negative answer were the true one, the positive inference 'then Socrates is unwise' is correct. But no such inference is correct in the case of universals, but rather a negative proposition. For instance, if to the question 'Is every man wise?' the answer is 'no', then the inference 'Then every man is unwise' is false. But under these circumstances the inference 'Not every man is wise' is correct. The last is the contradictory, the former the contrary. Negative expressions which consist of an indeinite noun or predicate, such as 'not-man' or 'not just' may seem to be denials containing neither noun nor verb in the proper sense of the words. But they are not. For a denial must always be true or false, and he that uses the expression 'not-man', if nothing more is added, is not nearer but rather further from making a true or a false statement than he who uses the expression 'man'."

Frank: He sometimes used the normal good-connotations of words above like: *evident*, *true*, *positive*, *wise*, *correct*, and *proper*. Words with bad-connotations included: *negative*, *unwise*, *false*, *contradictory*, *contrary*, *indefinite*, *not-man*, *denial*, and *nothing*, But it should be added that in the larger context of things these terms are so much like rather obvious value-*denotations*, like the expressions "good" and "bad" themselves that connote what they denote, that few of these words are very likely to prejudice anyone. More serious is that Aristotle commonly identified meaning with language, forms, and grammar rather than with intent, though as an exception he does seem to have acknowledged that *inference* is something human beings do and probably reflects a measure of human intent.

Frank: To the best of my understanding, it was John Stuart Mill who introduced the philosophical definition of denotation. He was a presentist who identified reality with sensations and who rejected causation in terms of influence in favor of successive or constant conjunctions among appearances, hence he saw nothing wrong with identifying denotation with reference or even with the notion that words mean when in fact in the real world, at least as most human beings understand the two mental processes, that is, association and reference, then particular persons both associate meaning with words and do the referring.

Frank: Let us now turn briefly to physical science and the question of Aristotle's position on falling bodies and friction. On the basis of everyday observation we can move small objects on a flat surface if they are not linked or tied to something, but after a while they will stop because of friction or counter-pressure from other objects, unless there is normally continuous pressure or from some place else to keep them moving. Aristotle's emphasis on friction was largely because he rejected atoms and the void and thought that matter is a plenum which fills earth and air such that friction while varying in degree was always locally present and can only be overcome by stronger force. But while Galileo's law of falling bodies and revival of the atomic theory have placed Aristotle's understanding in the shadows, this does not mean that friction is unreal or that vacuums are always easy to create.

Frank: Aristotle's version of less-idealized, eyeball physics, has been largely replaced in recent physics by many different assumptions and by much more idealized ways of thinking whose advocates are much more interested in understanding how idealized types of bodies fall to the earth under idealized conditions than how particular, real, individual objects actually fall when subjected to retarding factors from wind, atmospheric pressure, and other variables tied to friction at particular places and times. In short, Aristotle's physics while partly idealized is by no means as idealized as the much more mathematical approach of Galileo, especially in his law of falling bodies. On the other hand, Galileo as a defender of our particular historical earth revolving around a particular historical sun used a different conception of science which more closely reflects what I mean by doing less-idealized or non-idealized science.

Frank: On the other hand, one should note that Strato, one of Aristotle's own successors as head of the Lyceum, seems to have been the first to record natural acceleration when two rain drops began to fall at almost the same time from a roof while the farther they fell the distance between them gradually increased. But it would be Galileo almost two thousand years later who used that observation to develop his law of falling bodies which holds where gravitation is measurable, but becomes very idealized and one may add possibly even more dogmatic by making no mention of friction and by adding no qualification.

Frank: On the other hand, because Aristotle's reputation became so much greater than that of Strato partly because he discovered so many important and valuable things and partly because his authoritative, i.e. insufficiently qualified way of expressing himself, persuaded many readers that he was telling the truth, even when he was wrong. Aristotle's friction-focused physics generally prevailed for almost two thousand years.

Frank: When Aristotle distinguished between four different kinds of causes he also mentioned two types of motion, natural and unnatural. By making these distinctions, four causes and two motions, he was also distinguishing between different assumptions in terms of which particular types of cause and motion would seem more basic than the others. If an acorn was to become a flourishing oak tree, then it could be understood in terms of a *final cause* within the acorn to become an oak tree which was accompanied by *natural motion* or if one will by natural development. He also held that circular motion in the Heavens, and what we call gravitation were also kinds of natural motion, while *efficient causes* as what could prevent acorns from becoming oak trees were identified with *unnatural motion*. The other two kinds of causes material and formal, seem not to have been directly related to either natural or unnatural motion, though if one had to choose it would seem that formal causes were more compatible with natural motion and material causes with unnatural motion. As for recent idealized science it seems to have dispensed with or reinterpreted Aristotle's four causes while trying to restrict efficient causes to "mere common sense" in spite of its obvious priority when *doing* most observational, experimental, historical, or applied science.

Frank: Had Aristotle been asked whether he knew the truth with *unconditional* certainty, even he would probably have admitted that in spite of his normal use of under-qualified and hence dogmatic expression, that he was not unconditionally sure, and hence logically was only a *conditional* certaintist or high probabilist.

Frank: Some people like Aristotle, and many textbook writers have often lapsed into the habit of expressing qualification as little as possible, often it seems to save time and effort, but the search for truth should matter more.

Frank I think that the best philosophers are also historians. And the best historians are also philosophers. Nor are these just different ways of understanding the same thing. There are histories of philosophy, philosophies of history, histories of history, and philosophies of philosophy.

Frank: Because most historians don't understand philosophy or philosophers history, is my lecture likely to confuse students who only study history or only philosophy? I suppose so. It is true that I cannot do one without the other, and that is why I have to practice my lecture, again and again.

Frank: While Aristotle was long a leading theorist in rhetoric and was surely able to persuade some students of a logical or philosophical bent it is not always clear whether he was also a good speaker or orator, and, whether he was or not, whether he used rhetoric and what kind. Though one hears about his "golden dialogues", it is still hard to imagine that his emphasis on formal logic, syllogisms, and Enthymemes could attract or persuade listeners unacquainted with them and philosophy in general. One tends to think that writing was his vehicle and not practical oratory, though apparently as a kind of metic and not a born-Athenian perhaps he saw little need to use the kind of rhetoric in the Lyceum likely to influence "the common man", even if on a general or abstract level he did have a deep understanding of what could be effective in matters of persuasion.

Frank: The traditional defence of rhetoric is that it is one of the few ways of persuading uneducated or emotional people to accept the truth. But in what we now call a "democracy" where everyone should at least be educated well-enough to read and write one could argue that such means should not be necessary, but obviously they still are if weight of evidence is not strongly emphasized.

5

CICERO

Frank: Marcus Tullius Cicero (106-43) was primarily known as a Roman politician who as consul successfully opposed the Catiline Conspiracy and who attempted to restore the Roman Republic after the death of Caesar, but he was also a famous lawyer, orator, and writer of works in many fields including philosophy. His vast, extant correspondence is also valuable.

Frank: If no one thinks he is unconditionally certain of anything, then no one should be dogmatic in his beliefs. Or if one is conditionally certain or seems to be a conditional probabilist like Socrates, Arcesilaus, Carneades, Philo (or Philon), and Cicero. But a historically-minded philosopher, as we all should be, might ask: Who was Philo? The answer is Cicero's teacher in philosophy. But most philosophers have never heard of him, except perhaps for the best philosophers who may be for the most part also historians.

Frank: But where can we learn about him? From *The Oxford Classical Dictionary*, 3rd edition, 1996. And since many students don't have a copy, let us quote from an article by Gisella Striker on Philo in the 3rd edition which is also present in the 2003 printing:

> "In 88 [Philo left Athens] for Rome, where he numbered among his pupils Catalus, father and son . . . and Cicero who became his most devoted pupil and follower . . . Under the Scholarchate of Philon, the sceptical Academy modified its attitude . . . and adopted Carneades' account of the 'plausible impression' as an epistemological theory that would allow philosophers to accept the views they found most convincing with the proviso that [unconditionally] certain knowledge could not be achi-

eved . . . . It was probably in the two books he wrote in Rome toward the end of his life (84/83 B.C.] that Philon went a step further that knowledge was indeed possible, though not by the strict standards of the Stoic definition . . . In accordance with the new fallibilism of his school, Philon taught other philosophical subjects."

Frank: Philo also seems to have taught rhetoric which appears to have influenced Cicero. But since Philo's works have disappeared let us turn to Cicero's extant theory of rhetoric. See Cicero, *On the Good Life*, translated by Michael Grant, Penguin Books: Baltimore, 1971, pp. 237 and 241.

Some Advice on Oratory and Rhetoric

1. I have noticed that we do not quite see eye to eye! For what I like to argue is that effective speaking re-quires extremely wise theoretical knowledge; where-as you [Cicero's brother Quintus] prefer to maintain that oratory is entirely independent of systematic learning, and merely depends on a special kind of natural gift supplemented by practice.

2. So this, again, makes one appreciate how scarce orators are – and how scarce they have always been. And then consider the activity which we call by the Greek name of philosophy. You will recall that the most learned opinion identifies this as the creator and mother of every other noble art.

3. First, one has to acquire knowledge about a formidable number of different matters.

4. It is also essential to have an intimate understanding

of every emotion which nature has given to mankind. Other requirements include a certain sparkle and wit, and the culture appropriate to an educated man, and a terse promptitude in both repartee and attack.

5. A sensitive, civilized lightness of touch is also desirable.

6. One's memory too, must be capable of retaining a host of precedents, indeed the complete history of past times.

7. Nor is it by any means advisable to be ignorant of the law and existing statutes.

Frank: But even honorable and deep thinkers sometimes slip into dubious rhetoric and excessive use of value-connotation, Cicero is a conspicuous example. We would like to begin by praising Cicero for his attempt to defend what was best in the Roman Republic and for his late effort to write moderate and reasonable philosophy and encourage more Romans to write philosophy as well, and not leave it all to the Greeks. But he was also a lawyer and in that garb could be as rhetorical, prejudicial, and unfair as the worst mouthpiece or shyster.

Frank: Does the end justify the means? Presumably, yes, if both are ethical, effective, and have good side- and after-effects. But can an operational good bring us closer to ultimate good? *Is* there an ultimate good? Whether there is or not, I think the finest possible good supported by the most people and evidence should normally be treated *as if* it were an ultimate good or goal.

Frank: It is often said that no *is* implies an *ought*, but an *is* of purpose can at least seem to imply that something has at least operational value or goodness. For example, if my goal is to help a friend who seems to be drowning a short distance away, then it seems to follow that I *ought* to use the most effective means to help save him before he drowns. To be sure, one can imagine scenarios when I should not swim to save him if I cannot swim or if it is wartime and I am supposed to do my best to reach the other shore regardless of what is happening to my colleague, but under most circumstances the *is* of a friend drowning or seeming to drown does imply a moral *ought*. As for the formal objection that is-ought implication is merely approximate or ethical and not formal or applicable to all cases, and is particular and neither universal nor necessary in a strict sense, these objections appear to be irrelevant if meaning is based on intent and *should* be influenced by ethics. Some philosophers seem think that ethics is emotional and outside of reason and logic, but I think that there are probably several different kinds of value implication in general and ethical ones in particular, at least in terms of practical, non-idealized logic, and I have tried to suggest one or more examples. I also think that weight of evidence can be relevant or even decisive in helping to resolve many ethical disputes.

6

Frank: This selection is taken from four separate paragraphs within early pages of Cicero's *Second Philippic* against Marc Antony. Caesar had been assassinated, and Cicero acted as if there was a real opportunity to restore the Republic, if Antony could be defeated. Cicero writes as if he were directly speaking to Antony in the Senate, which indeed was actually the case in his *First Philippic*. (the term "Philippic" comes from the oratory of Demosthenes directed against the aggressive plans of Philip of Macedon toward Athens and Greece, but the

Macedonians timed their invasion successfully, especially after the Athenians had put extra financial resources into their social fund and not into building more warships and preparing a more effective army, a very different decision and result than had taken place against the Persians earlier). See Cicero, *Selected Works*, translated by Michael Grant, Penguin Books: Baltimore, 1965, pp. 105, 110, and 122.

"For what was left of [Republican] Rome, [you] Antony, owed its final annihilation to yourself. In your home everything had a price; and a truly sordid series of deals it was. Laws you passed, laws you caused to be put through in your interests, had never even been formally proposed. You admitted this yourself. You became an augur, yet you never took the auspices. You were a consul, yet you blocked the legal right of other officials to exercise the veto. Your armed escort was shocking [to us]. You are a drink-sodden, sex-ridden wreck. Never a day passes in the ill-reputed house of yours without orgies of the most repulsive kind.

Really, your speech was demented, it was so full of contradictions, from beginning to end You were not merely incoherent but glaringly self-contradictory: indeed, you contradicted yourself more often than you contradicted me . . . .

Would you like us to consider your behavior from boyhood onwards, Antony? I think so. Let us begin then at the beginning. Your bankruptcy in early adolescence – do you remember that? Your father's fault, you will say. And certainly such a filial self-defence! But it was typical of your impudence to go to the theatre and sit in one of the fourteen rows reserved for Knights, when the Roscian Law assigned special seats for bankrupts – and meant this to apply whether it was bad luck or bad conduct which had caused the bankruptcy. Then you graduated to man's clothing – or rather it was woman's as far as you were concerned. At first you were just a public prostitute, with a fixed price: quite a high one too. But very soon Curio intervened and took you off the streets, promoting you, one might say, to wifely status, and making a sound, steady, married woman of you. No boy bought for sensual purposes was ever so completely in his master's power as you were in Curio's. On countless occasions your father threw you out of the house. He even stationed guards to keep you out! Nevertheless, helped by nocturnal darkness, urged on by sensuality, compelled by the promised fee – it was through the roof, you climbed."

Value-Connoted Phrases

Negative: "what was left of Rome", "owed its final annihilation to yourself", "everything had a price","truly sordid series of deals", "blocked the legal right", "drink-sodden", "sex-ridden wreck". "Ill-reputed house", "orgies of the most repulsive kind", "speech was demented", "full of contradictions", "not merely incoherent", "glaringly self contradictory", "contradicted yourself more than you contradicted me", "your bankruptcy", "filial self-defence" (satire), "typical of your impudence","bad luck", "bad conduct", "public prostitute", "threw you out of the house", "urged by sensuality"

Frank: Cicero's effort to blacken Marc Antony's reputation in his *Philippics* was probably wise politics in order to help restore the Republic after the death of Caesar, and he almost succeeded. Unfortunately, the two Roman consuls who defeated Antony's army in northern Italy both died in the battle. The army then chose Octavian to be general, the young nephew of the recently assassinated Dictator for Life. And while the remnants of Antony's force retreated toward what is now Southern France, the defeated Caesarian was able to persuade Octavian to change sides, allegedly by quoting overly talkative Cicero that after the Republic was restored young Octavian as Caesar's heir would be marginalized. Antony and Octavian then advanced together on undefended Rome which allowed Antony to revenge himself on Cicero and have him murdered.

Frank: Even though the dead orator had ridiculed Antony's ability at public speaking there is evidence that Caesar's right-hand man could be even more effective than Cicero himself at persuasion, public and private. One remembers that he largely won the crowd against Brutus by holding the body of dead, bleeding Caesar in his arms in the Forum, and turned Octavian against Cicero. But while Cicero's skill at ridicule obviously may have helped to persuade the two consuls and initially even Octavian to oppose Antony, if we have the timing of events right, he was so extreme in most of the *Philippics* that what Cicero said was not so much considered to be literally true as to make Antony look like a despised laughingstock, but of course Antony had the last word. His later affair with Cleopatra also speaks for some capacity at persuasion, though she was also skilled at that. But persuasion by ridicule, exaggeration, lies, or beauty unless supported by strong, relevance evidence about what is very probably true and right can hardly be considered ethical, likely to be permanent, or far-seeing, as all three politicians, learned the hard way. Only Octavian died a natural death, but as the Emperor Augustus Caesar he apparently regretted having turned against Cicero in his later years, since he allowed most of his works to survive.

Frank: In the world of music, art, and literature, beauty can be important, and for Lucretius in describing the natural world in his famous poem it surely aided persuasion, but he supported his work with extensive evidence which is still widely accepted today. But in personal relations beauty can cause emotional addiction, which is often called "love", but is not rational or wise and often results in unhappy marriage or worse.

Frank: We probably need a new type of pill or medicine which can help reduce sexual attraction or at least the pain and suffering which occasional problems and frustrations may result, that is, if more people are to become more consistently rational, reasonable, happy, and responsible.

7

Frank: From a cultural point of view of literature, philosophy, and the arts one may speak of the highpoint of Greek Civilization occurring in the fifth and fourth centuries B.C., that of science in Aristotle's Lyceun in Athens and later in the great library and museum in Alexandria under the Ptolemies, and the Roman continuation during the first centuries B.C. and A.D. with Cicero as a leading contributor to several fields.

Frank: No emperors except perhaps Marcus Aurelius became as well-educated as many of the last defenders of the Roman Republic like Cato, Brutus, and Cicero. As for Christianity, less than a century after it was legalized, all other religions were forbidden. A century after that, the schools of Athens were closed and philosophy as free thought forbidden. For all of its ethical virtues, and we support them, the triumph of Christianity meant ideological dictatorship and the decline of reason, science, and the intellectual and cultural progress which the best Greeks and Romans had developed, defended, and died for. Unreason in the form of dogmatism as believing or claiming to believe beyond what the weight of evidence justified seems to have been the main culprit. Many philosophers tried to avoid that by relying on various kinds of probabilistic understanding like Philo and Cicero, but they were too few, and not influential enough.

Frank: Without high culture and probabilism, reason often seems to decline into scepticism as withholding judgment (Pyrrho), pseudo-scepticism as phenomenalist reduction (Sextus Empiricus), or open dogmatism as religious or philosophical over-belief. Christianity was not completely to blame for what happened or even barbarian invasions. Indeed, several barbarian generals became among the most skillful defenders of the Empire. Alas, to the best of our understanding, the Empire as permanent dictatorship had failed as a civilized and effective form of government primarily because of insufficient checks and balances on the choice and behavior of the emperors themselves, especially in the West, while religious concern for "the next world" which was not only a Christian obsession but shared by many other religions as well often weakened determination to defend the state, especially after St. Augustine in the early 5th century A.D alleged that one needed to have the Grace of God to do anything, active or good.

Frank: The Roman Republic in contrast to the Empire had limited legal dictatorship to emergencies and which must end in less than half-a-year, but Julius Caesar as Dictator For Life apparently did not understand why that office had been limited in time. But studying the fall of the Western Empire and the decay of high culture can help us master why that restriction was needed.

Frank: Nor was Cicero unreligious. He was loyal to the hope that there was a God and such loyalty made him pious in his philosophical works. But he did not think that belief which goes beyond what the weight of evidence justifies is either rational or necessary. In fact, if deliberate, such can be dishonest and hence a violation of religious ethics.

Frank: Most Romans including Cicero preferred a mixed state to prevent dictatorship by any person, group, or class, rich or poor. But in spite of his efforts and a relatively benign dictatorship under Augustus, the cultural decline soon began. More and more "free thinkers" became afraid to speak out. Rhetoric as style and flattery increasingly replaced the writing and publication of serious literature, though we should not forget the amount which would disappear during the rise of Christianity and the extended Dark Ages.

Frank: A rather unique side of Cicero came from his familiarity with Greek science, a subject which very few Romans outside of a few engineers had. Indeed, when in Sicily he did his best to restore the interest of the people of Syracuse in Archimedes, who for us and perhaps all scientists had been their most famous citizen. Cicero discovered that his gravestone had been forgotten and having been covered by weeds was even hard to find. He then restored it and did his best to honor him, even though in his day Archimedes had done his best to defeat the Romans in their siege of Syracuse. Cicero also wrote on astronomy in his book, *The Republic*, where he seemed to show interest in the theory of Philolaus, which also attracted Plato in his later years, that our earth and sun revolved around a central fire, a kind of double-sun heliocentric theory, but where being on the wrong side of the earth which Philolaus thought might not rotate on its axis except once a year prevented us from seeing the Central Fire. Nor was the geocentric theory as firmly held then as later supposed. There were several supporters of heliocentrism in the Ancient World, including Aristarchus of Samos and even the biographer Plutarch leaned in that direction as he also did toward the fallibilism of Philo and Cicero. It was hard, however, even for Cicero to take a double-sun theory very seriously but it did include movement of the earth around that fire, which was inconsistent with geocentrism.

Frank: In Cicero's later writings on government one sees that while he accepted both the Platonic notion that governments of small Greek city states often seemed to follow a circular path from monarchies to oligarchies to democracies to tyrannies and if the states lasted long enough perhaps back to monarchies again, and while he accepted the Platonic hope of using laws to help stabilize government, he of course rejected Plato's overly rigorous Republic in favor of his own model state based on what had been best in the Roman Republic.

 Frank: Cicero, began writing his *Republic* in 54 B.C during the triumvirate of Pompey, Caesar, and Crassus and was of course well-aware of how military leaders starting with Marius and Sulla had been subverting the Roman constitution, but in his book he went back to the time of the Gracchi brothers when the political decline seems to have begun. Nevertheless, he does not seem to have been fully clear about the social and economic changes which had made the old constitution less than fully practical. In a nutshell, Hannibal's initial victories reduced the number of small landowners who had been the backbone of the army and which under Marius had allowed anyone to become a soldier, while the military victories of the Late Republic added hundreds of thousands of prisoners to the population who became slaves and later freedmen but without traditional attachment to Roman values. The ex-prisoners of war increasingly worked in cities and on large estates for small wages until even more small landowners were disadvantaged, until they too began to drop into a large, frequently irresponsible underclass who often moved to the city of Rome along with immigrants from all parts of the expanding Roman state and even from outside and increasingly for "bread and circuses". Earlier, neither rich nor poor normally pushed their cause to the point of violence, but new leaders would frequently seem less restrained. Many Romans and later barbarians joined the army where some appeared to give more loyalty to victorious generals than to the Republic and its institutions.

Frank: Speaking of institutions, the Republican system like ours today had established numerous checks and balances to prevent dictatorship by one social class over another. The wealthier people had the Senate, the less wealthy had tribunes who could veto decisions by the Senate, at least once again after the attempted reforms of Sulla collapsed, and both rich and poor could vote for most high executive officials, especially the two consuls. Unfortunately, only citizens who came to the city of Rome in person could vote as in the old days but they were small enough in number, given the large number of slaves, freedmen, and immigrants who could not vote, so that enough local citizens could be bribed by ruling generals to choose many or most of the consuls and tribunes.

Frank: On the other hand, one could argue that there were too many checks and balances such that the legislative and executive branches of the Republic could no longer rule effectively and that the generals had to take over in order to accomplish anything important, but we think that if that were the main problem, then it would have been relatively easy to solve, since Sulla for example, in his reforms had reduced the power of the tribunes and censors, a major cause of gridlock, but since this step was widely viewed not as a way to make government more effective but primarily as a way of strengthening the rich against the poor it was soon revoked by ambitious politicians after Sulla's death to "restore balance", even if all it really restored was government paralysis. Needless to say, American writers of their Constitution, learning from Roman history, naturally agreed with Sulla on this point.

Indeed, late restoration of veto power for tribunes "to help the people" seems to have contributed significantly to fall of the Roman Republic, especially as understood in terms of Caesar's rise to permanent dictatorship.

Frank: An oddity was that the larger and more powerful the state became, the more slaves, freedmen, immigrants, and dispossessed small landowners flocked to Rome increasingly outnumbering the "real Romans" there, such that in sense the larger the Roman Republic, the weaker the central government became. On the other hand, since the system had demonstrated its ability by the remarkable expansion of territory and population in the first place, the recent fact that it was becoming drowned by an expanding underclass in its own capital suggested to Cicero that something must have worked almost too well over the previous four hundred years and that the unexpected problems which had arisen in the process could be handled and in a civilized and honorable manner. But since the Senate could no longer manage the vast numbers if indigents and debtors who needed help, without the risk of rioting and violence, ambitious military commanders increasingly took it upon themselves to settle their grievances before Cato and Cicero could discover how best to solve the basic problems in a legal manner.

Frank: When leaders in America wanted "to form a more perfect union" to rule a vast territory during the 1780's the only republican model they could find was the Roman Republic. They changed the two Roman consuls into one president and one vice president, kept the Senate, reorganized the popular assemblies, divided the nation into thirteen states with virtually independent governments in each one, and abolished the Roman notion of government tribunes and censors altogether, though newspapers would sometimes try to act as "tribunes for the people" and censorship has not been totally unknown.

Above all by adding a Bill of Rights as largely inspired by John Locke plus adding voting privileges to citizens in every state and replacing direct choice of candidates with indirect voting, one begins to see what supporters of the Roman Republic might have done to strengthen their state and help it survive much longer. Sulla tried with his heavy-handed reforms, while many Romans struggled to win support for a government of laws and not of men, but Caesar was too ambitious to let laws, especially the one against crossing the Rubicon river with an army, stop him. Nor could he seem to endure becoming a mere temporary dictator. He seemed to want total, permanent control.

Frank: But regrettably much as Greek-educated Cato and Cicero wanted to reform the Roman Republic, they could not see all of the needed changes which would be adopted in the American Constitution. It is of course foolish to see them as primarily leaders of an old aristocracy rather than as dedicated reformers who wanted to defend and improve republican government of a mixed kind, but such a mistake is natural among those historians who judge them adversely merely because they could not clearly see the best way to implement the needed reforms to help the government become more effective while keeping the needed checks and balances to prevent dictatorship. The old Roman Constitution had allowed for temporary dictatorships, but when Sulla was given dictatorial powers there was no temporal restriction, but as a true Roman he made it temporary by resigning after he had finished his reforms, but when Julius Caesar was made "dictator for life" it seemed obvious that given his love of power that unlike Sulla he would never resign. Thus, a plot developed to save the republic by slaying him. Indeed, no real lover of republican government in Rome or democratic government today thinks of a dictator for life as an acceptable solution. Sulla was as noble in this respect as Caesar was devious. On the other hand, Caesar was as generous and forgiving in personal matters with fellow Romans as Sulla had been harsh and brutal during his victorious return from Asia to Rome before he became dictator.

Frank: Cicero's book *the Republic* is imagined to take place in 129 B.C. shortly after Scipio, who had led the Romans to victory over Carthage in the Third Punic War, had begun a literary group to introduce higher intellectual standards into Rome, and even more recently helped defeat what seemed like an attempt by the elder Gracchi brother to overturn the Roman government and many of its institutions. Unfortunately, Scipio had married a sister of the Gracchi brothers, and Cicero apparently believed that she or her mother was responsible for Scipio's mysterious death also in 129 B.C. when he was only 56 years of age. But while Cicero considered Scipio to be the hero of his series of dialogues in *The Republic*, they were not designed like Plato's version to give a final answer but to suggest various possible solutions for restoring a viable republic. The Gracchi reformers may have hoped to help establish a more democratic and egalitarian regime, but what they got less than a hundred years later were civil wars and a succession of military dictators followed by Augustus Caesar.

Frank: Cicero's *Republic* while partly modeled on Plato seems to have been written to present government by experienced, practical men while philosophically representing the views of Socrates more than Plato to the extent we can distinguish between them. Socrates had criticized sophists largely because they seemed to reject truth as correspondence with reality in favor of a relativistic approach without that correspondence. But while Cicero is often considered a sceptic in what is called "epistemology" this does not mean that he rejected truth as correspondence with reality like the relativists, but merely our ability to be unconditionally certain about what is true, real, or right. In this respect he was closer as mentioned before to later developments in the Platonic Academy as represented by the views of Arcesilaus, Carneades, and especially Philo.

Frank: Since the primary goal of discussion where the search for truth is primary is *not* persuasion but to discover where the weight of evidence lay in the search for truth, then rhetoric should *not* be employed if it means an attempt at persuasion without supporting weight of evidence. Nor should it be assumed that formal logic can replace evidence, especially if it rests on dubious premises or idealized understanding of language, meaning, or both. Nor is the chief opposition another opinion per se, but *prejudgment* and *over-belief*, that is, dogmatism. Only when those two intellectual sins are eliminated, hopefully by weight of evidence, can real discussion start and deep analysis of underlying assumptions begin. In fact, just as the man of rhetoric whose goal is persuasion should not challenge strongly-held beliefs of an audience, so those who search for truth, for better understanding than what we have now, will often seem to *challenge* the beliefs of his audience by presenting weight of evidence, since if the challenge makes listeners and readers defend themselves even more strongly in spite of the evidence and its weight, then such people are clearly not yet suitable participants for serious discussion. Nevertheless, most persuasion in the absence of strong supporting evidence will often or normally lose strength over time, while challenging an audience by presenting weight of evidence may initially increase emotional opposition but should gradually work its way through until it is eventually accepted or at least tolerated or conditionally adopted, that is, with qualification.

Frank: Nor should we forget that even great orators like Demosthenes, Cicero, and our own William Jennings Bryan only persuaded a minority in a lasting way. Indeed, Bryan became the Democratic Party's candidate for president three times and always lost. Rational audiences are rarely held down long by emotional factors. And by reason we do not mean formal logic as pure reason, but practical reason supported by weight of evidence, the natural kind of logic we all have, and by appropriate qualification. The search for important truth should persevere long after first approximations have come to mind whether their source is rhetoric, formal logic, slanted research, unbalanced interpretation, or mis-evaluation of evidence.

Frank: One of Cicero's hopes was that other Romans would follow his lead and write philosophy in Latin. For example he asked Varro, perhaps the greatest Roman scholar of the age to help him create worthy Roman works on political and other kinds of philosophy or at least translate more from Greek. That prominent scholar replied, however, that the few people interested in such matters already read Greek. Nevertheless, one suspects that Varro as a student of Antiochus who had argued against Philo and in favor of a more dogmatic return to Plato had influenced Varro's negative reply. But the Dark Ages after the Western Roman Empire collapsed would reveal how knowledge of Greek in the West could almost completely disappear and along with it most secular knowledge in almost all academic disciplines. The Romans would simply neither translate enough Greek works into Latin nor write enough serious works in their own language to avoid the Dark Ages.

Frank: As already mentioned, Caesar, Brutus, Cato the younger, Cicero, Varro, and other Roman leaders had studied under Greek philosophers during the last years of the Roman Republic, along with many literary figures and poets, thus raising the intellectual level, probably above all other periods of Roman history, though the long reign of Augustus included

Livy and Virgil, and Marcus Aurelius and a few late Romans still used Greek, until the language itself almost disappeared in the Latin-speaking half of the Empire. To be sure, St. Augustine and a few early Christians could read some Greek, especially *The New Testament*, while criticizing many secular aspects of major philosophical scrolls, and even publishing their own books on sheepskin to distinguish them from many despised, unchristian works left on papyrus of which some were preserved in monasteries while many or most were allowed to disappear.

Frank: Speaking of Saint Augustine, it appears that a librarian in the Vatican in the year 1820 A.D. discovered that underneath a work by the Saint there was something else which had been almost completely rubbed out. But when modern techniques were applied, it became possible to read it, thus Cicero's *Republic* had come to life again, not all of it, but the largest fragment to be found yet.

Frank: The Gracchi had called for land reform, reducing the size of estates so that poor people could occupy and farm them, not an unreasonable proposal in an ideal world, but in the real world it meant taking land away from many senators and large land owners, and hence to do so fairly and effectively would require compensation and be done without violence and illegal procedure. Let us ask the question today: How many American or European landowners would accept such a proposal, especially if the law were passed illegally and with violence? This is not to deny that a *temporary* dictator in the long Roman history of such men, one remembers Cincinnatus for example, might have been able to redistribute land in a way to both preserve the republic and satisfy most poor people who might want to own and farm land to be transferred to them from previous owners, but neither the Gracchi nor the later generals, including Caesar, seemed willing to officially become a mere temporary, half-year dictator to solve the land and other problems, though Sulla did try to help and then resigned, while Pompey lacked Caesar's ambition and seemed happy to remain simply first citizen of the Republic.

Frank: Could a second temporary dictator after Sulla, but without his bloody past, have restored harmony and effective government in the Roman Republic? We do not know, but something analogous did work in Japan after World War II when General MacArthur and his GHQ became temporary dictators and broke up the large estates and distributed land to sharecroppers. They also broke up a large cartel of industrial businesses (Zaibatsu). After power was returned to the Japanese government, MacArthur's settlements seem to have been largely accepted, even the new constitution for Japan, though there has been occasional grumbling since then. On the other hand, it was surely easier for an occupying authority to do such things than in Rome with dug-in opponents both willing to use violence.

Frank: Still, there could have been a legitimate opportunity in Rome to use Ciceronian rhetoric to helps elect a temporary dictator agreeable to both sides to resolve matters, though whether it could have been done in six months might have been difficult. Naturally one thinks of Cicero himself as a "new man" being suitable for such a role or at least as an advocate for a reasonable compromise, but unfortunately his leadership against the Catiline conspiracy meant that he may have already been considered too partisan to be a neutral choice, though one naturally suspects Caesar's motives in trying to attract those of Catiline's followers and sympathizers who refrained from following their leader into his disastrous revolt and whether Caesar was genuinely willing to allow anyone apart from himself to occupy any important position which he could not control.

Frank: Cicero who did believe in fairness and good laws almost never accepted violent behavior contrary to law, except under extreme circumstances such as about the fate of Catiline and his followers, hence he opposed the Gracchi and their even less scrupulous military successors, but it is time to present a part of Cicero's *Republic* to see for ourselves. Since fairness to all reasonable perspectives and to the search for truth were primary in these dialogues one will see little rhetoric, except when participants were asked to present ideas or theories which they strongly rejected, and not always then.

Frank: On the other hand, we will find many value-connotations as such, associated with words and language. In short, demonstrating the use and application of good and bad connotations should help prove that language is not objective, but subjective, that is, what most people consider mental, and not only in its conceptual or spoken form, but in ideas and meaning associated with its written form as well.

8

From Cicero's *Republic* as trans-

lated by Niall Rudd, Oxford Uni-

versity Press, 1998

Book 1

Margin Numbers 10-11

"Again when they deny that a wise man will take part in politics, who I ask you, can be satisfied with their proviso 'unless some period of crisis compels him'? As if anyone could face a greater crisis than I had done [in the Catiline Conspiracy]. What could I have done at that time had I not been consul? And how could I have been consul if I had not followed from boyhood the career that would bring a man of [mere] equestrian birth like me to the highest office? So the opportunity of rescuing the country, whatever the dangers that threaten it, does not come suddenly or when you wish it, but only when you are in a position which allows you to do so. I find this most astonishing in the writings of intellectuals: they plead their inability to steer the ship when the sea is calm, because they have never been taught and have never learned to acquire such knowledge, and yet they will proclaim that they will take the helm when the waves are at their highest! These gentlemen openly admit, and indeed take great pride in the fact that they have never learned and do not teach anything about how to set up or maintain a government; they think that expertise in such matters does not befit learned and philosophical men and should be left to people with practical experience in that sort of thing. So what sense does it make to promise assistance to the government only if driven to do so by a crisis when they cannot manage a much easier task, namely to take charge of the government when there is no compelling crisis? Even if it were true that the sage does not voluntarily deign to descend to the technicalities of stagecraft, and yet does not shirk that duty if forced by circumstances, I should still think it quite wrong for him to neglect the art of politics: he ought to have everything at his fingertips, for he never knows when he may have to use it."

[Caesar and Pompey divided authority when this book was being written from 54 to 52 B.C., but this calm was soon broken by the civil war between them and the ascendency of Caesar afterwards, until his assassination in 44 B.C. Cicero was murdered by Marc Antony's men the following year.]

Words with value connotations

negative: deny, danger, threaten, inability, never, not…anything, crisis, sage (satirical), deign to descend (satire), shirk, wrong (a value-denotation), neglect.

positive: wise, satisfied, rescuing, steer, calm, knowledge, gentlemen, fact, teach, maintain, expertise, practical, sense, assistance, take charge, true.

10
From Book 2
Margin-Number 10

"How then could Romulus have achieved with more inspired success the advantages of a coastal city, while avoiding its faults, than by founding Rome on the banks of a river which flowed with its broad stream, smooth and unfailing, into the sea? Thus the city could import by sea whatever it needed, and export its surplus; and thanks to the same river it could not only draw in by sea the commodities most necessary for its life and culture, it could also bring them down from the hinterland. So Romulus, in my view, already foresaw that this city would eventually form the site and center of a world empire. A city founded in some other part of Italy could hardly have held so easily such vast political power." [There is some poetic license here. Virgil would treat Aeneas the Trojan as the founder of Rome. When the

132

barbarians came in the 5th century A.D., Ravenna would tend to be a more secure ruling city, and of course, Constantinople would prove militarily more defensible than both Rome and Ravenna. But Cicero could hardly have anticipated these things in his day.]

Words with value-connotations

Negative: faults,

Positive: achieve, inspired, success, advantages, smooth, unfailing, thanks, life, culture, foresaw, center,

11
From Book 3
Margin Numbers 8-*11*
(Two leaves are missing.)
"PHILUS: What a splendid case you are putting in my hands, when you ask me to undertake the defence of wickedness!

LAELIUS: Still, if you make the points which are usually made against justice, you needn't worry about giving the impression that you actually believe what you say. After all, you yourself are an absolute model of old-fashioned honesty and good faith; and everyone knows your habit of arguing both sides of a case, because that, in your view, is the simplest way of getting at the truth.

PHILUS: Well, all right then. I'll play the game your way and deliberately cover myself with mud. That's something that gold prospectors don't shirk: so I suppose in digging for the truth, a thing far more

precious than all the gold in the world, we shouldn't try
to avoid the consequences, however nasty. I only wish
that, as I am going to use someone else's argument, I
could also use someone else's mouth. As it is, Lucius
Furious Philus will have to say the things that
Carneades (used to assert), a Greek fellow who used to
devise verbal arguments for whatever was expedient . . .
"

Words with value-connotations

Negative: splendid (satire), wickedness, against
justice, mud, so I suppose, nasty, devise, expedient.

Positive: model, old-fashioned honesty, good faith,
simplest way, truth, gold.

Frank: In spite of heroic efforts by the editor and translator of
Cicero's *Republic* to find passages in other Ancient works to
fill in the missing pages of the last three chapters it is still not
possible for us to follow our plan of using random selections
based on the tenth margin-number of each chapter or "book"
any further. Nevertheless, we end our selections from Cicero
with a short quotation from him preserved by a good historian
from the late 4th century A.D., Ammianus Marcellinus (30. 4.
10) a great admirer. It is remarkable in that it suggests that
Cicero and through him one of the speakers in his *Republic* was
aware of and strongly regretted that members of his own
profession of law and their use of rhetoric possessed serious
capacities for evil.

"Nothing in a state should be so free from corruption as
a vote and a verdict. So I fail to understand why a man
who corrupts them by money [like Caesar?] should deserve punishment whereas one who does so by elo-

134

quence should actually win applause [like Marc Antony in the forum on the death of Caesar?]. For my own
part, I think that a man who corrupts a judge [or the
public?] by his speech causes more harm than one who
does it by a bribe, for no honest man can be corrupted
by a bribe, but he *can* be by eloquence."

12

Frank: Though I am not always a good example, I wish we had
more research-focused historians and fewer thesis-historians,
especially those who fail to study enough evidence against their
amour propre. But it is possible for many of us to read the same
basic works, study the same evidence, and have the same major
goals so that we can sometimes reach the same conclusions.

Frank: History of course is important but I did not realize it
could be used to help understand other fields in a basic way like
rhetoric and semantics until it was tried. In addition, no science
or scientific research could last long without historians to
describe and preserve what scientists are doing and have done,
and given the reliance of all science on many earlier historical
developments. Also, it would be unkind, unfair, and
unchivalrous to deny that historical writing is often very
scientific in its attention to detail.

Frank: I think it is more certain that Columbus crossed the
Atlantic several times, than anything that is objectified or
idealized. And if the more certain, the more scientific, then it
could be that at least some written history is the most scientific
field of all, but in the absence of reliable evidence or when
historians disagree with colleagues simply because they use
different sources of evidence, which in a way is a reflection of
insufficient research by both parties, then history may often
seem to be the least scientific of disciplines.

Frank: Still, no one knows all of the fields which describe themselves as sciences or their reasons for doing so, hence attempting to define science is almost certain to be premature and too narrow. Idealization as either over-simplification or as gilding the lily is not a virtue about the real world.

Frank: One has also learned that historians often consider this writer a philosopher while philosophers identify him with historians, but almost no one links him with semantics his first love, but hopefully these dialogues could help change matters. Nevertheless, he keeps looking for someone who can appreciate all three fields: semantics, philosophy, and history.

Frank: As tastes improve, we hope to find new readers, especially since we have tried to remain free from fashions. It used to be said that every age has to rewrite history to fit current ideas, but it is possible to maintain the contrary, that some books are written for the ages, precisely because one avoids becoming overly attached to recent points of view.

Frank: No one knows our fate, but the world does know how lasting and attractive the works of Homer, Plato, Lucretius, Tacitus, Plutarch, Marcus Aurelius, Bacon, Shakespeare, Descartes, Montaigne, Locke, Byron, Keats, Shelley, Tennyson, the Bronte sisters, Balzac, Hugo, Shaw, and many other classics have been and remain for all generations. On a more technical level works by Aristotle, Archimedes, Galileo, Newton, Lavoisier, Faraday, Planck, and Einstein will surely continue to find readers from many scientists and historians of science.

Chapter Four

SEMANTICS

Vera: Are you against science?

Frank: No.

Vera: Then why do you seem to criticize mathematical science so often?

Frank: Because many mathematicians who philosophize tend to advocate the use in most or all science of idealized methods which only some scientists sometimes use and which discriminate against non-idealized science.

Vera: So you are really critical of certain types of mathematicians and philosophers of science?

Frank: Yes.

Vera: Why?

Frank: Because I think a more realistic type of semantics based on actual causes as influence can and should help reduce their support of unnecessary idealization. I think people mean and not words, sentences, propositions, and languages, useful as these traditional habits of association sometimes are.

Vera: Can you give an example of idealization.

Frank: Yes. Starting in the Ancient world, it became widely accepted among many mathematicians, especially followers of Plato, that all celestial motions were circular. Thus, even though what appeared from earth to be planets did not actually move in circles, but sometimes seemed to reverse their direction into what was called retrograde motion, and that outstanding astronomers like Hipparchus and later Ptolemy felt obliged to introduce fictional deferents and epicycles to give the impression that the apparent planets really did move in circular fashion. In short, they used an idealized method to help misunderstand real particulars like earth and the planets, instead of idealized types of things under idealized conditions where idealized methods can at least sometimes be legitimate.

Vera: How was it discovered that apparent planets were not the real planets?

Frank: First, because light through the atmosphere close to the surfaee of the earth is displaced such that the apparent planets near the horizon are not where the real planets should be. Second because retrograde motion of apparent planets is not plausible, regardless of mathematical fictions to make their orbits seem round. And third, because the heliocentric theory and the earth revolving on its axis can easily explain the retrograde motion of apparent planets without adding more fictions and idealizations.

Vera: Could you give a more reeent example of how mathematicians or philosophers have introduced deceptive idealization, especially into semantics?

Frank: You are really asking more than one question, but I will do the best I can. As mentioned before, the philosopher, John Stuart Mill, during the 19th century, is commonly credited with introducing the notion that the denotation of words meant what the words referred to, but an opinion closer to reality would sbe that if to cause means to influence in a spatial or temporal way, then it is more reasonable to assume that human beings refer to objects as part of a mental process of thinking rather than that mere words carry out the process. But if true, and if connotation is the process of human beings associating ideas and feelings with words, then it would seem that both connotation and denotation suggest that meaning depends primarily on people as if basically people mean and not words, sentences, propositions, or language.

Vera: In other words, as if dictionaries and conventions give an idealized conception of meaning, first, in terms of causes as if impotent laws were causes, and second, which apply to normal or *types of situations* and not necessarily to people using language in *particular situations* at particular places and times? And if all reality is particular in that way, then relying on idealization or fiction about semantics as theory of meaning scarcely seems reliable enough about what is real to deserve to be considered fully scientific.

Frank: Yes. But I have no objection to idealization if it is fully admitted to be such, if it is only applied to idealized types of things, and if the mathematicians and philosophers who support it will have the decency and fairness to acknowledge that non-idealized science also exists and not only in biography, history, and psychology, but in observation, experimentation, and much applied science as well.

Vera: Nor can we reduce science, philosophy, semantics, the physical world, or accurate understanding of anything to a mere "physical object language" or to any mere language for that matter.

Frank: Indeed, linguistic philosophy itself seems to be a mistake, though one can imagine a possibly reliable philosophy about the use of language, though even here some mathematicians and philosophers may still try to introduce unnecessary idealization and misleading presentism.

Vera: I have vaguely heard about a controversy between General Semantics and Logical Semantics during the Nineteen-Thirties. What was that about?

Frank: Many writers supported meaning as intent and tried to turn it into a movement which eventually was called General Semantics. It was first suggested by ideas from Lady Victoria Welby to find ways to improve communication by analyzing different uses of the word "meaning". It was taken up by G.K. Ogden and I.A. Richards in their book *The Meaning of Meaning* which first came out in 1923, but which did not give as much credit to Lady Welby as she deserved.

Vera: Can you give me names of those who supported meaning as intent?

Frank: F.C.S. Schiller, the pragmatist and relativist about truth; S.I Hayakawa who later became a senator from California; Stuart Chase, an economist who wrote *The Tyranny of Words*, which influenced me as a teenager, and then there was Alfred Korzybski, a Polish aristocrat, an original theorist, but not very skilled at persuading enemies who he falsely thought were potential allies. Both Logical Positivism and his own movement were young in the 1930's and because he wanted to make his semantic movement a science, he thought he could persuade the positivists to join him.

Vera: But didn't Carnap and other positivist writers become his strongest opponents!

Frank: Exactly. But he had trouble understanding why, which brings up the difference between a theorist and a deep philosopher. Korzybski had lots of interesting ideas but did not seem to be very conscious of his own underlying assumptions which he largely took for granted and did not seem to clearly express, while what I call a deep philosopher, and not just a theorist with a philosophy, does know his own basic assumptions or at least a lot of them.

Vera: What didn't he know?

Frank: That he was a fallibilist and indirect realist who extended his doubts to formal logic, while many academic philosophers, mathematicians, and logicians who were the backbone of Logical Positivism at that time did not. In fact, the new mathematical logic was largely on the top of their minds plus an extreme empiricism which following David Hume they thought they could reconcile with extreme formalism.

Vera: But weren't they also fallibilists?

Frank: Many to a large extent were, but that did not normally include mathematics and formal logic. But there was a bigger difference too. The positivists, like us all, valued certainty, but while to some extent many members did distinguish relative from absolute certainty, they did not fully grasp that if absolute certainty means *unconditional* certainty, which is not a rational notion, then their conditional fallibilism should have been extended to accept Korzybski's more complete if largely implied version, but of course as "professionals" they refused.

Vera: How did you discover K's extreme fallibilism and his indirect realism, if they were rarely expressed as such?

Frank: By re-reading Max Black on K's attack on Aristotle, which seemed to presuppose K.'s fallibilism and K's notion that our nervous system limits us to inference about nature.

Vera: Thus something perhaps too obvious for K to be expressed, but either overlooked or rejected by the "pros" was the sticking point and helped rally positivists against him?

Frank: I think so. They knew he questioned Aristotle's often dogmatically expressed views on formal logic, but confident in the new logic, many positivists either could not take Korzybski's understanding of Aristotle seriously or they recognized that he was a fallibilist about all formal logic, which clashed not only with their confidence in the new logic but with Wittgenstein's revival of dogmatically expressed philosophy.

Vera: So either formal logic or unlimited fallibilism?

Frank: So it apparently seemed to many frightened Aristotelians, logicians, positivists, and mathematicians.

Vera: Assuming they took their opponents views seriously in the first place.

Frank: The chief weakness of intent-based semantics which in the minds of many people seems to have merged with Korzybski's General Semantics was that apart from Schiller none of the supporters appeared to understand philosophy well-enough to accurately distinguish friends from foes, and Schiller who did know who his enemies were was not sufficiently young, tough-minded, or long-lived enough to lead the movement, but also because he was in England and the movement was in America. He was good at understanding many aspects of practical reason, but one must add that his pragmatism and relativism could also seem objectionable because of their opportunistic character and proclivity toward the use of rhetoric.

Vera: How did Logical Semantics develop?

Vera: But first, I think you may be guessing about K and why the logicists opposed him. I think they thought he was a crank from the start. But I would like to be clearer about the nature of Logical Semantics.

Frank: John G. Kemeny, a professor of mathematics, who wrote a long article on Logical Semantics for the *Encyclopaedia Britannica* (1964), hence not too long after the controversy, began his article by making a typical distinction of those days from Rudolf Carnap between pragmatics, semantics, and syntax and alleged that "Semantics in logic aims at the building of an abstract theory of the relation between signs and what they mean." (The symbol "K" in this dialogue is for Korzybski.)

Vera: And by thinking of laws as causes and not historical influence, they could take abstractions more seriously than their more practical opponents who inferred from causes as influence that only what was concrete was real.

Frank: Yes, the author, a mathematician, defended the notion that signs (including words) mean because to quote: "ordinary (natural) language is hopelessly complex because of the fact that its syntactic structure is not precisely determined and that it employs many ambiguous and vague expressions. Hence, Logical Semantics deals only with fully formalized languages" unless of course one argues like most General Semanticists and many Linguistic Semanticists that by focusing on the likely intent and assumptions of speakers and writers that much ambiguity and vagueness can be overcome, that is, by studying relevant history and psychology.

Vera: Then how could Logical Semanticists have won the debate?

Frank: They didn't really win. They linked intent-based semantics closely with Korzybski's ideas, misunderstood them, and then "refuted" what they had misunderstood, and later accused him of being a crank as if he were irrational. It was another strawman type of thing. No real person or movement was refuted, and certainly not his anti-rhetoric allies, but I admit that the larger academic community imagined that the positivists and formalists had won, but of course without understanding that the issue really turned on whether logic and mathematics were unconditionally certain and should be considered exceptions to unlimited fallibilism.

Vera: What turned the tide against Korzybski??

Frank: Perhaps a *Britannica* article on Logical Semantics. The author, Max Black, an admirer of Reid's rather dogmatically expressed presentism, criticized K's position on Aristotle without relating them to K's fallibilism and representism.

Vera: You are also an unlimited fallibilist, but I am sorry to have to admit that I am still a fallibilist about fallibilism.

Frank: Korzybski published his major work *Science and Sanity* in 1933, the same year Black published his tome: *The Nature of Mathematics – A Critical Survey*. Like most people, Korzybski naturally assumed that people who believe or claim they can be absolutely or unconditionally certain (like Black?), are not only probably mistaken but not fully sane. Korzybski was wounded in the First World War and had hospital experience in both Russia and the U.S., where he came to regard over-belief and dogmatic claims as symptoms or signs of mental illness.

Vera: But what were his actual views in a *detailed* sense?

Frank: According to Black, K argued that 1) Aristotle used either-or logic 2) confused the "is" of identity with the "is" of being or existence 3) only allowed two truth-values i.e. supported an excluded middle in logic, 4) confused symbols with what they symbolized, such as a map with what it represents, and 5) accused Aristotle of basing too much on the law of contradiction.

Vera: I can see why Aristotle scholars might take offence.

Frank: As a fallibilist, 1) I think K was right to oppose A's frequently expressed dogmatism as if he could not be mistaken, since even if Aristotle's best understanding was more qualified than his expression, his dogmatic words could still help dogmatize many of his more gullible students into over-belief. 2) I am not sure how often A confused the "is" of identity with that of being in either expression or intended meaning, but even once would have been too frequently. 3) fallibilists rightly qualify truth-claims to allow that what seems to be possible may need to be expanded beyond either-or and two-value restrictions, 4) presentists like A often fail to distinguish between what representists in epistemology like K mean by mental symbols which represent something physical, while presentists commonly treat the symbols themselves as if they were the external objects and there is no representtion, except between ideas and appearances, and 5) as mentioned earlier, since no rational person intends a contradiction, when it is or seems to be expressed it is almost always a verbal or merely accidental mistake, such that instead of criticizing it like A often did, it is normally wiser and kinder simply to try to determine what the victim of potential or actual criticism most likely intended.

Vera: What kind of correction did Korzybski (i.e. K) suggest dogmatists needed as under-qualifiers and over-believers?

Frank: He advocated what he called "therapy" and called the medical condition of dogmatism as over-belief along with the practice of over-generalization "un-sanity" and suggested that the tendency either to believe or to generalize beyond the weight of evidence as an illness could be partly cured by the use of "indexing" individual persons with the same name like John$_1$ and John$_2$, different years when something important happened[192], and he proposed use of he term "etc" when something more is intended in a series but left unsaid or unwritten. Such practice may help people who generalize too much or too frequently, but may not help over-believers, especially in mathematics or formal logic.

Vera: I admit that over-belief may contribute to dogmatizing and illegitimately persuading students, and hence can act as a kind of rotten rhetoric, but I still think logic is fundamental in all rational thinking, and that over-belief in it may still be preferable to bad logic or attempts to reject logic or do without it.

Frank: I agree, but natural human logic is different from formal logic, and primarily needs resistance to prejudice, over-belief, rhetoric, and what Bacon called "idols" in order to thrive. Indeed, Bacon and Locke supported natural logic but not formal logic in their campaign against traditional Scholasticism which was still being taught in many European universities. It is the false theory of meaning and semantics which formal logic rests on which is the problem, the notion that words and propositions mean and not particular persons at particular places and times.

Vera: Thank you for the explanation.

Frank: Like most human beings, I do hold that people who think they can be certain in the sense of unconditional certainty are sick, that is, if unwilling to admit that they could even possibly be wrong or mistaken. They are not just probably in error, but are mental cases as well, and could use the right kind of therapy, if it can be found. But of course many mathematicians and logicians who over-believe in the certainty of either the old or the new formal logic may not be willing to admit that they are sick or even mentally disturbed, and hence may resent K's theories in the extreme, especially about the need for therapy, and could well be inclined to fight him and his theories tooth and nail.

Vera: I think that their conception of possibility is narrower than your fallibilism-enhanced version, or the one you attribute to K on the basis of Black's description and which could be interpreted to be unlimited, even if one does acknowledge that many things are probably true or real and that nature may well have existed before there were animals or human beings and whether we know anything about what it was or is in an unconditional sense.

Frank: I agree.

Vera: Which also means that the formal logicians with their more restricted notion of possibility could well seem to over-believe or over-generalize from the perspective possibly of Korzybski and more definitely of yourself. Those logicians who are violently unwilling to even think of therapy or reform would naturally reject Korzybski as a crank, and possibly including you as well, as if it were Frank and possibly K who were sick and needed a medical "cure".

Frank: While Korzybski would have been too civilized and rational to reciprocate by calling anyone a "crank".

Frank: After his failure to persuade Logical Positivists to become fallibilists in his sense and therefore more rational, reasonable, and responsible, he might have still wanted to help cure their mental illness by putting them under therapy.

Vera: I think you are joking. They might have killed him if he had tried to do that.

Frank: True, but please don't misunderstand me. Many positivists were serious about wanting to objectify language, and meaning, approach unconditional certainty, and they really thought that idealization was objective or could help provide it, though they should have known that if something must be real to be either objective or subjective and that what was merely objectified or idealized like "a physical object language" was not even real in a literal sense, let alone objective in any significant way. Nor was it easy for them to demonstrate that propositions themselves were more than mentally objectified fictions.

Vera: I can sympathize with Korzybski when observing patients after he became injured and his wish to expand therapy to dogmatists, that is, to over-believers, but when most philosophers still reject scepticism more than dogmatism and even identify probabilists like you with scepticism as if absolute certainty were possible, then K's good will and plans for basic therapeutic help for mental patients suffering from over-belief or a tendency to over-generalize was almost certainly doomed from the start.

Frank: But the dirty game was played by philosophers like Max Black who not only declared or implied that Korzybski was a crank as if K's basic assumptions and many of his ideas made other than good sense, while blatantly ignoring that the main thrust of general semantics was an attack on the use of misleading rhetoric, like what the positivists and Logical Semanticists were so often guilty of doing, and have not yet fully refrained from doing.

Vera: Why not concentrate more on recent philosophy?

Frank: Dogmatic speaking and writing helped make Aristotle seem like an authority in many fields where he was wrong, and has helped make much modern philosophy unreliable as well, starting with many semantic aspects of Logical Positivism and

Analytic Philosophy such as their notion that words and propositions mean, and not human beings, though of course they occasionally do give lip-service to some of the ideas of their own more reasonable semanticists like Herbert Paul Grice.

Vera: You mean that as long as over-belief remains uncured, that regress in philosophy is always possible and may even currently exist, which suggests that even the deepest foundation theory, which could conceivably even resemble your own, may only be just one more stage of development doomed to be replaced, and most likely by something inferior?

Frank: Real philosophers try to discover and improve upon the deepest assumptions we have …

Vera: but which may be too unclear to fully decipher let alone understand, while minds that introspect less often about fundamental, non-idealized matters may tend to prevail.

Frank: They already do.

Vera: Let us return to another topic.

Frank: Which one?

Vera: Why you switched from Berkeley to UCLA.

Frank: Some things are better forgotten.

Vera: Or more exactly, how did Berkeley philosophers prevent you from getting a doctorate at that time?

Frank: Many of them thought I supported Korzybski, approved of his fallibilism, and rejected unconditional certainty, even about the new formal logic and the ideas of Carnap and Wittgenstein.

Vera: But you did! Their criticism was true!

Frank: Let us say their identification was partly correct.

Vera: How many angels stand on the head of a pin?

Frank: Not as many as they thought. I had read books by several of K's allies, but his book *Science and Sanity* was very heavy and hard to read, and I never finished it. I did mention it in a speech class and the reception was somewhat similar to the introductory dialogue to the series of them in this book which hopefully some one will be reading soon, but it never occurred to me at that time that he was as much of a fallibilist and conditional probabilist as I was.

Vera: Where had you first studied that perspective?

Frank: I first studied the position carefully as a freshman at the University of New Mexico in 1950 in a sociology class where the teacher gave us the dialogues of Plato to read. I especially liked the early one where Socrates said that "I only know that I know nothing". That was probably a main source of my own opposition to dogmatism, not Korzybski, who I had not even begun to read until the next year and never understood well until Black's description and his lack of insight about what it meant woke me up to some of K's probable assumptions.

Vera: If Black and initially you had trouble understanding K, then why have most academics supported Black against K ?

Frank: Because B may have presented the kind of criticism they wanted to hear. Perhaps they didn't want formal logic to be criticized. Nor had they thought through the issue of conditional versus unconditional certainty or the fact that formal logic rests on many conditions, especially about the nature of language and meaning. Also, many readers blame authors for unclarity.

Vera: I still doubt your new interpretation of K's 1933 book, especially about his alleged fallibilism. You may be reading your own views into his.

Frank: Possibly. I entered the University of California in 1955 after two years in the Air Force, and became a graduate student in philosophy the next year, but I was weak in foreign languages and spent 1957-58 in Freiburg im Breisgau learning German, but in those days each department gave its own language exams and when I returned to Berkeley I was given Husserl to translate at a time when his works had not been extensively translated into English.

Vera: And you failed?

Frank: It was hard not to because Husserl used a lot of Greek words which I did not know, and in the middle . . .

Vera: and then?

Frank: Someone entered the exam room and loudly declared that I had failed the French exam.

Vera: Did he know you were taking the German test?

Frank: I am not sure, but I suddenly realized that each department had a private way to eliminate unwanted students.

Vera: How could you be certain?

Frank: I went back to Germany to learn the language better, but when I re-applied to return to Berkeley they told me my grades were not good enough, even though I still had a B average.

Vera: Why were you in effect kicked out?

Frank: I strongly defended Socratic questioning and of my fallibilistic position in Berkeley. They also called me a supporter of K who was already considered a crank by most philosophers.

Vera: So you think that the popularity of Wittgenstein's rather dogmatic *Tractatus*, your doubts about the new mathematical logic, and the insistence of some of your professors that fallibilism may not apply to formal logic were relevant factors?

Frank: Perhaps, but I did take the logic course using Quine's difficult text and received a good grade, though even then I had no desire or plan to ever use or accept an artificial language as a substitute for natural language and meaning as human intent. It still seemed scholastic and pointless to me, and with my fallibilism and view that nothing was unconditionally certain, I naturally could not accept the view that formal logic as something idealized, scholastic, and based on bad semantics was the heart of philosophy or could ever hope to be unconditionally certain. As you know, I was still much influenced by Bacon, Descartes, and Locke, and could not see any serious merit in Berkeley, Hume, or Kant and their return to presentism in their rejection of what I considered to be the real physical world beyond sensory appearances.

Vera: Why did you read more history of philosophy than the contemporary stuff?

Frank: You just answered the question yourself. Most of it is transient, though Nancy Cartwright is not dogmatic about laws.

Vera: Were you ever an assistant at Berkeley?

Frank: No, but I was a grader, which I enjoyed. In a class of about two hundred I was assigned to grade a question about Descartes, but I took so long I was fired.

Vera: Why did you take so long?

Frank: Because I saw no point in simply giving a grade without explaining to the student, if his answer was insufficient, what was wrong and what a better answer would have been. The question was to clarify Descartes *Cogito ergo sum.*

Vera: But if there were two hundred students, then it must have taken a month!

Frank: It did, and the students liked it, but the professor didn't.

Vera: How did you support yourself?

Frank: We needed part-time jobs in those days, especially after my G.I Bill ran out. Though some good students had scholarships.

Vera: Did you mean "good" or good students?

Frank: I don't like to generalize on insufficient information.

Vera: Unless proper qualification is intended or expressed?

Frank: Right, and in this case it would have to be both intended and expressed.

Vera: And then you switched to UCLA, a branch of the same university system, which also initially accepted you as a graduate student in philosophy?

Frank: But there was an ironic result. I took a course on Husserl, but because there were still not enough English translations of his books, the professor had to teach the students enough German to understand Husserl, but he excused me from his class because I "already knew too much German".

Vera: So you never did read Husserl?

Frank: Not true. I did.

Vera: I'm sorry. I should not have said that.

Frank: Please forget it.

Vera: But this time there really were grade problems?

Frank: Yes, but you are right that I did not enjoy his type of over-belief and under-qualification any better than that of Wittgenstein. Nor did I like Husserl's prejudice against psychology in favor of intuitional logic, which often seemed like reified fiction to me.

Vera: What kind of philosophy courses did you take at UCLA?

Frank: Plato again, and I also took two courses at UCLA in epistemology which I thought was my strongest modern field. But the professors identified that branch of philosophy not with the recognized positions in it, but as theory of immediate or absolute certainty. Both also held and taught presentist views and would not recognize my representist position as being certain enough to qualify as genuine epistemology, and when I realized this I tried to transfer out, but it was too late. I desperately studied harder than ever and even tried to become more sympathetic to the three books by Logical Positivist A.J. Ayer, which one of my teachers had insisted we all read carefully, but when I finished both courses both professors gave me a grade of "C+", which for a graduate student was a failing mark.

Vera: And then you transferred to history?

Frank: Yes, but there was an interesting story while I took the other epistemology course. Many students were still enthusiastic about Wittgenstein in the early sixties, especially about his posthumous book on "linguistic families" as if context influenced language and meaning. One day in the seminar I mentioned that his student Miss Anscombe had published a book called *Intention* in which she appeared to support meaning as intent. This did not surprise me, since anyone who studies language closely would naturally come to such a view sooner or later and also that Wittgenstein's switch from a words-mean convention to his new semantics also represented a step closer to the people-mean position and which his assistant had recently taken. But many students in the seminar were surprised and began to become seriously interested in her book. The professor, however, wondered how one could be certain about what another person intended, presumably meaning what could be absolutely or unconditionally certain.

Vera: I realize that it may be hard for a person with unpopular views to remain absolutely silent in a seminar, but maybe you should have tried it some time.

Frank: Have you ever done it?

Vera: No, but if I did maybe I could have stayed out of trouble more often than you did as a student.

Frank: I of course defended my probabilistic approach, but by then it became clear that in his eyes I was rejecting epistemology itself, while for me, I mostly meant by the field of epistemology the differences between the various schools of presentism, like phenomenalism, idealism, and direct realism and the different schools of consciously indirect epistemology like representism and Platonism and not about the issue of knowledge as absolute certainty. The question by the professor plus the students' switch in interest from his concerns to those of Anscombe and her new book on intention told me that he was angry and that my goose was cooked in that class. Instead of the required single paper for the only grade given in the seminar, I wrote an extra-long second paper in the hope that the professor might forgive me, but nothing apparently could stop him. I was shot down like K apparently had been by philosophers who rejected unrestricted fallibilism along with meaning as intent, regardless of how much more reasonable they have seemed to me and to numerous other people as part of a sound world view.

Vera: But your philosophy includes much more than that.

Frank: A bit more, yes. Support of Vaihinger's *Philosophy of As If* added an element needed to help make fallibilism more practical, but that largely remained my private interest, since the only thing many philosophers apparently knew about him was his interpretation of Kant. Indeed, after his death his journal was taken over by the Logical Positivists, but that only helped confirm that all change is not necessarily an improvement.

Vera: And about the transfer to the history department at UCLA?

Frank: I became happy in L.A. My four doctoral fields Greek History, History of Science, and both Early Modern and Late Modern European History were allowed to be subordinated by kind history professors into a single discipline close to philosophy called "Intellectual History". Grades of "A" and nothing below a few "Bs" came easily, the language exams were no problem, largely because the university and not individual departments now gave them, and after two years I passed my preliminary exams and began to write my doctoral dissertation, which took four years and would become over a thousand pages long on a controversial scientist-philosopher. Twenty-eight historians received doctorates in my last year at UCLA, but only two were given "With Distinction".

Vera: And you were one of them?

Frank: Yes.

Vera: But if the rather large history department was so much more congenial than the much smaller one in philosophy, then why did you eventually go back to philosophy with its interminable conflicts?

Frank: Because I still thought my philosophy was more reasonable than their alternatives, which I still do.

Vera: At first you were a semanticist, then a philosopher, and finally a historian, especially a historian of science, but semantics and philosophy seem to have remained your life's mission, even though many professionals in those fields remain as determined to stop you as ever.

Frank: The other academic and scientific interests are all linked to semantics and philosophy, and are understood largely in terms of philosophy, or more accurately, foundation theory.

Vera: Perhaps we should change the subject.

Frank: It's not so easy . . .

Vera: When personal factors are involved?

Frank: I think fairness also includes recognizing one's own fallibility and mistakes and not dismissing improbabilities out of hand. In short, let us both stop acting as if we were always right. We should be more than pots calling kettles black, and in both semantics and philosophy, not to mention history, science, religion, and sociology.

Vera: I don't object to calling kettles black if what I notice still looks black, two wrongs never make a right, no one is perfect, and truth is not altered by our own imperfections. Effective *action* is based on the highest probability wisely treated *as if* certain.

Frank: And wise *understanding* is based on considering many different possibilities and selecting the one most likely to be true, while respecting and keeping in mind many which are less likely, but where a turn in the weight of evidence could restore the fate of theories and ideas from improbabilities into becoming probable or even very probably true.

Vera: There may be degrees of probability, certainty, and even belief, depending on weight of evidence, but referents are either real or unreal and correspondence with reality is either true or false. I still believe in logic, and not of a merely sentimental kind where we try to be generous and considerate to unintended but expressed contradiction, circular argument, and other faults of reasoning, since minor flaws can have major consequences.

Frank: But if errors of expression and reasoning are not fatal to one's basic point, then it would be unethical and unfair to emphasize them. I also respect logic, that is, when based on intended and not on objectified or idealized meaning.

Vera: Many still prefer deductive argument to evidence.

Frank: I criticized Carnap for that reason. Evidence does need judgment, but when relevant and strong should be preferred.

Vera: Was Carnap still at UCLA then"?

Frank: No, but he was till in the area, but had retired.

Vera: And you knew him?

Frank: In my long dissertation I interviewed many scholars and philosophers who had known the person I was writing on or who held opinions about him, and he was perhaps the most illustrious.

Vera: But you have also implied elsewhere that he was only half-educated, and harsh to his wife, and the result was . . .

Vera: A book defending him . . .

Frank: which put positivists on their guard against me?

Vera: Biting a hand that helped you is not ethical.

Frank: His help did not go very far.

Vera: You were envious and bitter because his ideas won followers and influence and not yours.

Frank: Perhaps, but when Rudolf Carnap still maintained: "The concept of reality (in the sense of independence from the cognizing consciousness) does not belong within (rational) science, but within metaphysics". See page 282 in *Logical Structure* (1969) while he was still active, I felt that Carnap either did not know that Galileo, Newton, Planck, and Einstein, probably the greatest physicists of all time, held exactly that "metaphysical" view in or underlying their science during their mature years, or that he knew and was lying. Nor did his "physical object language" replace their indirect realism Nor could language or "construction" determine or replace meaning as human intent. He seemed to prevail with falsehood.

Vera: Yes, he may have been as slippery as William James when alleging that mere consequences could determine truth and value. But your criticism showed weakness of character, and will be criticized. Think ahead to advancing beyond the ideas of both James and Carnap and to more recent and daunting challenges.

Frank: As a historian it is hard to leave the past uncorrected.

Vera: I prefer to reform the present with insight from the past.

Frank: I am willing to seem weak and envious for accusing him of moral faults. But someone had to do it, and that person should properly have been a historian.

Vera: But as a philosopher it is irrelevant if about epistemology, ontology, or methodology of science. And if his ethics was not spotless, then neither is yours for bringing it up.

Frank: I was also disturbed by his defence of objectified meaning, though such an attitude as his was and is still widely spread among logicians and mathematicians. Nor as is well known did he give full credit to Wittgenstein for many ideas while in Vienna. He was a womanizer during his years in Prague, at least according to his longtime admirer Friedrick Herneck, who helped me a lot in my own research. And it seems likely from Carnap's Nachlass in the University of Pittsburgh in America that his wife was neurotic, and according to the widely respected philosopher, Charles Hartshorne, that Carnap was not always nice to her before her suicide. If it is immoral to criticize immoral actions, then I am guilty, but is it?

Vera: Please stop. We both know you made a mistake.

Frank: I always thought philosophers should live their philosophy like Socrates and Confucius. Putting personal living out of bounds may be fine for what Thoreau called "university philosophers", but a prominent leader like Carnap should have tried harder to transcend presentism, dubious morality, and neo-scholastic love of formal, that is, idealized understanding. His rhetorical skills helped him mislead other philosophers into rejecting "metaphysics" i.e. foundation theory, real philosophy.

Vera: What did Carnap look like shortly before he died?

Frank: He had a noble beard and looked thin, very unlike his pictures, very aristocratic, but because he still defended objectified meaning, communication was difficult, since he would not discuss underlying assumptions or how he might be wrong. He wanted disciples, not the kind of deep analysis I thought was needed.

Vera: You took the matter too seriously

Frank: He let sensory and idealized truth satisfy him, even though a very close childhood relative of his had been a famous historian of Ancient Athens and familiar with non-idealized understanding.

Vera: But some of my fellow students may be worse, since they lean to relativism about truth, often as if relativism and fallibilism were the same or as if relativism merely meant that truth was approximate.

Frank: Yes, I even remember a girl in one of my classes, who decided not to study "because truth was merely relative".

Vera: She was wrong.

Frank: And young. I should have told her then that fallibilism is compatible with holding that truth means correspondence with reality, but that relativism about truth is not.

Vera: I would have told her that if truth were relative then she didn't exist and that there was no point in trying to talk to her.

Frank: Greek sophists like Protagoras are said to have held that "man is the measure of all things" and Carnap that using "a physical object language" could be objective or replace trying to understand the real world in a non-idealized way.

Vera: Why didn't you study elsewhere and get away from Carnap's influence?

Frank: I did when trying to learn German, but as a graduate student with an address in California I could only afford to study at Berkeley or UCLA where his teachings increasingly prevailed over the thinking of deeper minds from an earlier era like Arthur Lovejoy and George Santayana.

Vera: Did he persuade by soft-soaping logicians and mathematicians?

Frank: Largely. They were his main audience among "philosophers".

Vera: Please don't continue! No more sour grapes. That was over fifty years ago. It is better to forgive and forget.

Frank: That is what I keep reminding myself, but it was you who wanted to hear about my inglorious past.

Vera: I partly regret asking you now, but it does help explain why you are capable of being so hard on human byproducts who have evolved from the positivist era in philosophy.

Frank: You are right, and I apologize if I exaggerate their influence on contemporary thinkers.

Vera: By rejecting the very idea of rhetoric, you may have made it impossible to win debates against such people.

Frank: No. If I won, which was often, they resented it, but lacked the character to either admit it or change their opinions

Vera: No one wins debates in philosophy, unless the defeated party admits it, which I have tried to do with you.

Frank: a kind thought.

Vera: No, but I do try to be perceptive and learn.

Frank: In practice, I almost always use rhetoric and logic chopping more than I should, especially since I do not believe in them. A history professor said that I lacked self-discipline and an education professor that I should never admit personal faults before my students. I have tried to discipline myself better but I am rarely a good teacher for two reasons, first, I teach what I like and not what they want, and second, what I think they need is a broader outlook, hence my courses seem rather shallow or scattered to them. Both professors were probably correct from a practical perspective, but lasting reform is another matter.

Vera: At first, I wanted to know your personal past, but I didn't realize how painful that period was. You must not identify success with the reaction of others. You survived and can still exert influence on future semantics and philosophy. Please overcome personal defeats and keep fighting, but not against people.

Frank: I often try to be objective and refuse to answer most false accusations against me, but they keep coming and coming from Carnap's die-hard supporters, and now, even some non-positivists believe them.

Vera: Future research will expose false judgment, and I will always defend your depth and wisdom.

Frank: Which can help sustain strong resolve in the semantic struggle to come against both rhetoric and prejudgment.

Vera: Good, but please keep struggling hard for truth, not to repair personal wounds.

Frank: I also knew Sir Karl personally.

Vera: And that relationship was good?

Frank: At first, I sent him a copy of an early book, and he liked it, since he knew many of the Viennese professors mentioned. I then visited him, and he tried to help me publish a book, and I offered to write a full-scale biography about him which no one had yet written up to that time. When he finally thought the matter through, he rejected my offer since he correctly claimed that I did not understand the roots of his philosophy well-enough, his underlying motivation, and that it would take me a decade to master his basic point of view.

Vera: Please stop. I am no longer curious. Pandora's box is shut. Your personal life is out of bounds.

Frank: And Popper was right. It did take a decade until I saw that his main goal was to persuade historians and non-mathematicians to accept that all science was idealized and that scientific language and meaning were objective as well.

Vera: I see, while Carnap captured many students already inclined toward mathematical science, Popper tried to round up the rest, especially non-mathematicians, to support idealized science and idealized language and meaning about science.

Frank: I was blind for years. I admired Popper for so many things such as his fallibilism, opposition to linguistic philosophy, his indirect realism about the external world, and especially his almost Socratic, critical attitude, but naturally opposed his attempt to reduce causes to mathematical laws, his extensive use of prejudicial terms, his frequently misleading rhetoric, and his fictional "world 3" as a sop for over-believers in the alleged reality of abstract fictions.

Vera: His main goal appears to have been to persuade non-mathematicians, including historians like you, to accept what

most logicians and mathematicians accept? And when he saw
that he couldn't possibly persuade you in the long run . . .

Frank: But even then, I could not accept his view that history is
unscientific because allegedly either we rely on "unscientific
laws" or try to use no laws at all, when in fact we normally
think of causation in terms of detailed influence and don't need
general or universal claims in the explanation process, largely
because abstractions do not seem influential enough to be real
for us. We also tend to presuppose what we mean by free will,
that is, we attempt to *will* to follow our best understanding *free*
from slavery to the passions.

Vera: While most people mean free will as being free to do
whatever they want.

Frank: Which describes slavery to the passions for us, the
opposite of real freedom.

Vera: The Stoics often tried to obey your definition, but you are
far too emotional and even sentimental to make a good stoic.

Frank: Popper of course looks for freedom *to* instead of
freedom *from* and like many physicists contrasted freedom with
deterministic laws instead of with slavery to the passions, in
short, by freedom he did not really mean freedom of the *will*.

Vera: Is it possible that he declined to have you write an
authorized biography because he feared you might discover
something deep but embarrassing?

Frank: I don't think so, but he did suggest that I write an
unauthorized monograph, that is, without access to his notes
and correspondence, but please, no more talk about such things
He was an open, honest, and somewhat argumentative man, not
totally unlike myself. But he may not have realized how

strongly many historians are against idealization, laws as causes, and the notion that language and meaning are objective, or *why* we reject abstractions as causes.

Vera: Is everything real concrete?

Frank: For me, yes; for him, no. There is a difference between concrete particulars and abstract types. Narrative history as science normally focuses on the former and mathematical physics as science on the latter, but unfortunately many scientists and philosophers only seem to focus on mere sensory appearances and abstract types. I think both Carnap and Popper erred, but I made few efforts to persuade them and was not gifted in the types of rhetoric likely to succeed.

Vera: So if you couldn't do it well, you turned against rhetoric and the philosophers who employed it more effectively than you?

Frank: I was always been opposed to dishonorable reasoning from the age of sixteen when I first read Stuart Chase's book *The Tyranny of Words*, but did talk too much in my futile efforts to persuade other people. Would I like to learn how to persuade better, yes, but only if it means mobilizing and presenting stronger weight of evidence more often and in a clearer and non-misleading manner, that is, not by tone of voice, style, reputation, dogmatism, or other dubious, irrelevant, or less than open and honorable methods. In terms of my best understanding, I would rather fail than cheat to win through rhetoric or emotion in spite of retaining a strong will to help sound semantics and other wise aspects of foundation theory prevail.

Vera: But no one can always follow his best understanding, or even know what it is.

Frank" But when I try to use what I think is our best understanding about the issues we have been discussing, it becomes clear that we have not allowed for enough exceptions on both sides of semantic and philosophical issues. All positivists are not over-believers in formal logic, and we ourselves use more rhetoric than we should and don't always qualify our judgments enough.

Vera: Many mathematical scientists and philosophers also become more historically-minded and reasonable as they become older.

Frank: Nor do all historians identify causes with influence and what is concrete or all sociologists generalize when they should be doing more research into relevant particulars.

Vera: Philosophers often rightly distrust inductive generalization, and even when historians qualify it down to something accurate, its significance may also be reduced.

Frank: But I still hope to see more respect for non-idealized understanding by more mathematical scientists, philosophers, and others who tend to take extensive idealization for granted.

Vera: What additional changes would you like to see?

Frank: I think we should distinguish more carefully between pure and practical reason. Logicians and mathematicians often undervalue non-idealized science based on practical reason and what largely rests on it like historical research, careful description, and good judgment.

Vera: You mean by practical reason: inductive logic, means-end logic, and cause-and-effect logic?

Frank: largely.

Vera: But they only give probable truth at best, and even that is conditional.

Frank: Which is often more reliable in the real world than what is merely true under idealized conditions.

Vera: I don't think the issue is which type of reason has more application in non-idealized science, but whether mathematical science can do without pure reason and idealization.

Frank: Though from their perspective they don't always see what idealization is or that it even presents a problem, since they commonly look for what is most simple with the most inclusive scope and often as if exceptions and qualification were something to be avoided, since they make it less likely that one has found a genuine law or constant.

Vera: But idealization doesn't just work in abstract science; it is indispensable.

Frank: The world has changed. In the macro-realm physicists often noticed an appearance and tried to infer what was actually the case and then used measurement to help prove it, but now that the micro- or sub-atomic world is the main focus one often develops ideas like string theory, quark theory, and spin up, spin down theory, as if science were mostly abstract theory.

Vera: Idealization is better than nothing.

Frank: But something is better than idealization.

Vera: Repeating an argument does not make it more true.

Frank: Or less true.

Chapter Five

CONNOTATION

Belle: I hope I can help you better than I did Frank. He thought he could prepare his lectures better without me.

Vera: He's a bit touchy sometimes.

Belle: No, it was more than that. He is so in love with the Greeks and Romans that he cannot accept modern improvements in philosophy.

Vera: Maybe he doesn't think they are improvements.

Belle: But those old guys, especially Plato and Aristotle, engaged in metaphysics. Plato believed in something called "Forms" which are neither empirical nor truly mathematical and also his *Republic* over-organized social and political institutions to such an extent that even many students of Marx like it.

Vera: And Aristotle?

 Belle: His physics is notoriously qualitative and unmathematical. And Frank defends those people.

Vera: Maybe he thinks other aspects of their philosophy are better.

Belle: Better or not, they are not comparable with modern philosophy.

Vera: I recently talked to Frank and he apologizes for . . .

Belle: kicking me out? He should. I was only trying to help him become acquainted with recent thought. He is so wrapped up in the past.

Vera: Would you like to hear what he said?

Belle: No, but to please you, I'll listen, a little.

Vera: He was sorry that he was too busy to give you the response you deserved.

Belle: He said that? Let me hear more.

Vera: He said you were a quick thinker.

Belle: I try to be.

Vera: Which is good for training in much science.

Belle: And recent philosophy of science?

Vera: Not exactly, but he also said that some fields require consideration of many points of view before reaching even provisional judgment.

Belle: I prefer intuition.

Vera: He fears mistakes in trying to do that, so he wants to think s l o w l y, c a r e f u l l y, a n d w i t h a l o t of q u a l i f i c a t i o n.

Belle: And I rushed him?

Vera: He thinks you are more suited for training than education.

 Belle: Now wait a minute. I studied Plato and Aristotle when I didn't have to. I also like breadth and so-called "education".

Vera: So-called?

Belle: Yes, if education requires considering a lot of different possibilities and fields in a v e r y s l o w way before even venturing provisional judgment, then it is mere armchair stuff, dithering before doing. His approach is too mentalistic and psychologistic.

Vera: But you did it, and liked it.

Belle: It was a mistake. Maybe recent philosophy of science is more training than education, like science itself. So what? Its still better than metaphysics that calls itself "education".

Vera: No. You learned, for example, that Plato had a theory of Forms. That was a good first step.

Belle: I learned a lot of *other* things too.

Vera: Did you learn *why* he held that theory?

Belle: If I did, I forget.

Vera: If you had understood that, it would have been a second step from learning to understanding and from training to education.

Belle: Now I remember. He was impressed by Pythagoras and number mysticism via Philolaus and a trip to Syracuse.

Vera: If you understood *why* Plato accepted a theory of Forms in spite of it seeming mystical to you, then a clever student I know would have understood even more.

Belle: And become even better "educated"? You're a good friend, Vera, but scientists *reject* why questions and so do I.

Vera: If they can't answer them, yes, but in the real world, if something unexpected happens or the expected does not, then even most scientists ask why, just like everybody else. Why-questions ask for explanation, and without explanation there may be learning but little or no understanding, and without understanding there is no education.

Belle: If I have to ask why questions like children do all the time to become educated, then I prefer to remain a specialist or mere trainee, as long as its in science. "Why mommy? Because I told you so. … Why because? You wouldn't understand. Why wouldn't I understand?"

Vera: Okay, you made your point, but missed the real point.

Belle: Which is?

Vera: Inquisitional persistence.

Belle: I prefer to burn at the stake.

Vera: That's only for relapsed heretics.

Belle: Like Joan of Arc?

Vera: Any visions lately?

Belle: Lots of them!

Vera: Did Aristotle accept Platonic Forms?

Belle: No. He was critical.

Vera: Why?

Belle: I don't remember.

Vera: The more you can answer why questions in a true and informative way, then . . .

Belle: like children, every answer can provoke a new why, until we fall into an infinite regress.

Vera: Only in theory, not in fact. Answers take time and we don't have infinite time.

Belle: I renormalize infinities, like the physicists do.

Vera: It might be easier to reject the convention that dividing zero into a real number gives infinity. By pursuing questions farther, and not just asking a single why, we can often learn and understand more about our own assumptions and those of other people, and by improving upon them we may become well enough educated to approach developing a wise foundation theory, a deep and profound philosophy.

Belle: So all I have to do to "understand" instead of merely learn, and to become "educated" instead of merely trained, is to ask a lot of stupid why-questions and then introspect?

Vera: No, there is much more, including research and evidence. We need lots of relevant information to be able to answer why-questions in a trustworthy and informative manner, especially about causes as both plans and implementation, and we should qualify answers so that they will become more understandable and sound. For example, is it good to reject their ideas before understanding why Plato accepted forms and why Aristotle criticized belief in them?

Belle: I guess not, if we look at the matter seriously. I'll try to be more inquisitive, even if it threatens endless mommy-nagging.

Vera: Especially then, at least until we understand why the ideas of many individual Greek thinkers should be studied.

Belle: No one can ask or read everything, and it is natural to think in most fields that what is latest is best.

Vera: Even about philosophy?

Belle: Science advances, and current philosophers want to advance too.

Vera: Can we understand anything in a deep way without considering earlier thought?

Belle: Perhaps not fully.

Vera: Is it fair to study past thought using current criteria?

Belle: What else is there?

Vera: Understanding what Plato meant from his own perspective.

Belle: But what if it is false?

Vera: Only after asking a lot of questions and studying a lot of ideas from many thinkers from then till now, are we likely to be able to answer that question, and even then our answer will be or should be conditional and hence only probably true at best.

Belle: And like Frank you think that meaning is in the intent of the speaker.

Vera: Yes.

Belle; While most positivists and analytic philosophers think that language and meaning are objective.

Vera: Right.

Belle: Which you think are superficial movements?

Vera: Or at least insufficient for maximum communication.

Belle: About past *and* present thinkers?

Vera: About understanding and not just learning.

Belle: Is all training indoctrination?

Vera: If not queried or challenged it can be.

Belle: So philosophy is not just one more field dominated by training?

Vera: The most basic, rational assumptions in all fields are philosophical.

Belle: Some philosophers want followers more than truth.

Vera: Most recent ones are relativists.

Belle: Or what Plato called sophists?

Vera: Almost. Nor should one confuse relativism in physics with relativism about truth.

Belle: I suppose I should amend my position, but it is more fun to harass stuffed girdles.

Vera: I think you know what Frank's advice is.

Belle: Since I put speed and happiness first, he probably thinks I should go back to science or at least to a field where hasty judgment is less fatal.

Vera: Does that mean less dead?

Belle: Yep! Like Schrödinger's cat.

Vera: We both think you are bright as a button, but hope you will slow down, admit mistakes more readily, and depend less on training and more on education, research, and reflection, but given your personality . . .

Belle: I *can* change. No more haste or prejudgment!

Vera: Even about recent thought?

Belle: That too. I do want to become educated, even if I have to become more inquisitive and wear diapers. By the way, What is your latest project?

Vera: To list very prejudicial terms, and explain why we need to expose them as intellectually dangerous. Less prejudicial terms can persuade without our knowing it, but extremely prejudicial expressions can frighten many people into de facto acceptance through fear of being painted with the same brush. For example, many philosophers claim to reject metaphysics, even when they don't know what is meant except that the connotation is bad. They are reluctant to resist such prejudicial terms through dread of being accused of being "metaphysical" themselves.

Belle: What does "metaphysics" mean?

Vera: Originally it was used as a name for a book by Aristotle alleged to come before or after another book about physics. More recently anything which is neither sensory nor formal, all kinds of occult, religion, mysticism, ontology, theory of reality, reality, trans-conscious reality, and more or less everything we disagree with or have trouble understanding. In short, except in very restricted circles, it has acquired like its adjectival form "metaphysical' a very abusive, all-purpose, bad-connotation that still means many different things to many different people, that is, when as denotation it still means anything different from its value-connotation at all. Honorable philosophers rarely use the word, except to warn students *not* to use it.

Belle: But you and Frank criticize it all the time, as if you both had a secret purpose.

Vera: Yes, our purpose is to help more people consider the full range of possible philosophy *without pre-judgment.*

Belle: Like Scholasticism, positivism, and formal logic?

Vera: Frank has to try harder than normal to be fair to them.

Belle: And you?

Vera: In my better moods, I can also be fair.

Belle: And which type of metaphysics do you like best?

Vera: Indirect realism in epistemology, mind-matter dualism in ontology, and clean handkerchiefs for snotty students in philosophy of life.

Belle: I'm sorry; it slipped out.

Vera: As Cesare Borgia would say: "Slip it in fast, between the ribs."

Belle: I thought that was Brutus?

Vera: He did it to save the Republic, just as his namesake had killed the last Roman king.

Belle: I'm getting out of my league. Wasn't Plato an indirect realist and Descartes a mind-matter dualist?

Vera: Yes, though people who believe in atoms are also indirect realists, and the direct realist, Thomas Reid, was also a mind-matter dualist, so there are a lot of different points of view which we would like to protect from premature and unfair criticism.

Belle: What would sound better than "metaphysics"?

Vera: Almost anything.

Belle. Like what?

Vera: "Potential candidates for foundation theory."

Belle: But that just reverses the value-connotation?

Vera: Not all the way, I called them "candidates", not necessarily part of the final solution.

Belle: That sounds ominous.

Vera: By no means! I am feeling better! Please try this beautiful red apple. The taste is unforgettable.

Belle: To be fair to old metaphysics could be interpreted as denying that recent philosophy has made significant progress.

Vera: Fallibilists think we should keep possibilities open, and in a fair and unprejudiced way, that is, if we are to ask, research, and wisely judge our way into deep or profound understanding of what is true, real, and right.

Belle: I think I will try a different apple.

Vera: Words with bad-connotations, like "metaphysics", are bad apples, and can prejudice your way into error and falsehood

Belle: What about words with *good* connotations?

Vera: They can also lead to prejudgment, but because most people like to hear words with positive associations, the slant is often overlooked, with a common result being, wishful thinking. You are too intelligent and pretty Belle to surrender to academic and social fashions of the moment.

Belle: I like to be flattered, but how much of your talk is true?

Vera: Let us start with epistemology, not as "metaphysics" or theory of knowledge which as alleged immediate acquaintance or unconditional certainty may not be legitimate, but where different philosophers start by drawing a line between mind and matter as if mind can normally be made conscious but not matter even though both are real and both can be influential.

Belle: If they exist at all.

Vera: If everything scientific or real could be made conscious, then any division would have to be within that scope and would make differences between what is mental and physical rely more on different relations than on irreducible types of qualities.

Belle: I'm sorry that's too technical for me, especially since so many current thinkers seem to reject everything mental or opt outside of epistemology for a so-called "physical object language".

Vera: If only what is conscious to a particular person were real, then he would risk falling into solipsism, since he would seem to be alone, since he is not conscious of anything beyond his own impressions. It was largely for this reason that the belief arose that language if it were objective and used by everyone could logically both get us out of solipsism and provide an objective foundation for science.

Belle: But what is wrong with that?

Vera: It is not true. Neither language nor meaning are objective They are subjective processes in our head and can vary substantially from person to person.

Belle: I suspect you are defining "true", "language", "meaning", and "subjective" differently than most analytic philosophers.

Vera: That is so, but does not change the facts. Are you willing to try to understand these differences in order to understand *why* different people draw the line in different places and hence have different basic philosophies?

Belle: Only when intimidated by wiser heads.

Vera If we draw the line between mind and matter where Descartes, the acknowledged founder of epistemology, drew it, that is between what is real and is or can be made conscious, that is, the mental world, and what is also real but cannot be made conscious, which is the physical world, then we can begin to make progress in our understanding of man and nature

Belle: But my teachers did not stop there. They rejected Descartes', mind-matter dualism.

Vera: Because many philosophers did not accept his argument that a trans-conscious external world has to exist "because God would not deceive us."

Belle: Which still seems weak, even if not to some religious people.

Vera: I think Descartes' real reason came from the representative theory of perception which was widely accepted in those days and from a careful study of optics and physiology.

Belle: So you agree with Pascal that Descartes was not really religious?

Vera: No, because what Pascal meant by "really religious" may have seemed casino-oriented and bizarre to most Christians.

Belle: Will it help if I attempt to t h i n k   m u c h   m o r e   s l o w l y ?

Vera: Most people take for granted today that what can be influenced by prejudice and emotion is subjective including and also allow that intent-based understanding can be relatively objective which when combined together can be a source of your attack on rhetoric and "illegitimate persuasion". But I think you should be more careful in your own use of language. "Relative objectivity" as something precarious does not always mean the same thing as "relatively objective" which suggests partial or a degree of being objective or something comparative.

Vera: Your way of speaking suggests the normal dictionary approach as if words had meaning and even the old Aristotelian and updated notion as if so-called "propositions" could mean or have meaning.

Belle: Frank would be happy that I learned something from Aristotle, excuse me, *understood* something, i.e. took "a third step" toward education.

Vera: One should not be cynical about education. It is a kind of rational liberation which can make us happy.

Belle: Was Diogenes educated?

Vera: In twisted terms, but I don't think he was happy.

Belle: Why not? His jar kept out the rain.

Vera: Without clothes he needed the sun, which Alexander blocked.

Belle: Fashionable ladies still go half-naked, and no one blocks them. Diogenes was a pioneer, a true naturalist.

Vera: That's not how the word is normally used today.

Belle: I remember. Instead of "The word means" we should say "Frank associated a denotation and a value connotation with the word before he used the word to help refer to my interruptions."

Vera: Why not just say "Frank means" which is often true even when he doesn't use words or other symbols at all?

Belle: Because only you "really" know what he means?

Vera: That's not fair, and it is largely because people mean and not words that *Roget's Thesaurus* is often more useful than both dictionaries and watered definitions, especially of "objectivity". People often have an idea or meaning in mind, but cannot think of just the right word, and both meaning and the words are mental and hence can be made conscious, at least in principle. And hence in a good sense are subjective.

Belle: I have already heard too many words during my first two decades.

Vera: We all need a thesaurus on occasion.

Belle: My computer has one, but I forget where it is on the machine.

Vera: Most people use it because they forget a lot.

Belle: Only geezers like Frank.

Vera: And they also learn many new words.

Belle: Next, you will want me to "understand" them, whatever that means.

Vera: Would you like to understand how a thesaurus works?

Belle: No. Even dummies can read the index.

Vera: Would you like to see my list of bad words?

Belle: Yes. Its hard for girls to catch up to boys.

Vera: They are not really bad words. They merely have value-connotations, of which some are good and some are bad.

Belle: Oh! But if I have to seem curious to become "educated", then go ahead.

Vera: You should try harder to really get interested!

Belle: Will education help me become president?

Vera: It could make it possible.

Belle: I think learning rhetoric and "illegitimate persuasion" would help more. Ha! Ha!

Vera: As more people become educated they will demand higher standards.

Belle: Than your list of words with value-connotations?

Vera: A much longer list than mine, much longer. People can be taught not to use value-connotations to help persuade or to be persuaded by them.

Belle: Okay: let's see what you've got.

Vera: Its just a list of samples. But before I begin, I have to discuss a series of different kinds of relations between meaning and expression.

Belle: "Why"? See, I remembered to ask Frank's favorite unscientific question. I am not doomed to be a mere scientist who is only trained, nay indoctrinated, who never understands anything or can hope to be educated like grand ladies who write down lists of words with value-connotations.

Vera: I am not grand, and if you keep it up, I'll demonstrate that I'm not a lady either by pushing your face in. Now stop it!

Belle: But educated friends of Frank *don't do that*. Furthermore, by using satire I proved that tone of voice can change or even reverse meaning, which you both should appreciate in your campaign to prove that meaning is mental.

Vera: I'm sorry he hurt your feelings, but you are young and educated enough to get over it. Use your best understanding!

Belle: Thank you. At least one person thinks I am educated.

Vera: We can all study more and become *better* educated, even Frank.

Belle: Good! I'll stop tormenting his sidekick.

Vera: You do have a way of getting under people's skin.

Belle: I don't understand.

Vera: Oh don't you! The most drastic disconnect in semantics is between words and inaccessible meaning such as in a dead language where no one knows either the pronunciation, tone of voice, or what their users intended or meant to communicate.

Belle: And secret codes also disconnect intent and expression?

Vera: Until they are broken, though the people who invented the code or who have a code book should be able to decipher intended meaning, even if expressed words or symbols initially seem to be no help.

Belle: You mean that one has to clarify all that *doesn't* affect value-connotation first before one can notice it?

Vera: No. I mean the opposite, that a thousand-and-one ways to use words in addition to satire can trump the value-associations normally made with words.

Belle: Then why are those connotations so important?

Vera: Because by far the majority of words are used in a familiar language where value-connotation can and often does help prejudice people into believing what is true is false.

Belle: Or false is true.

 Vera: False arguments can be challenged, but value-connotation is so often overlooked that it can count more victims.

Belle: But it only applies to individual words.

Vera: Most sentences include several individual words.

Belle: But as you say underground communication, shorthand, and mathematics can normally obscure most value-connotation?

Vera: Underground communication like that in the Soviet Union before its overthrow is somewhat like a secret code. Shorthand requires someone who can read it, but value connotation may also be associated with shorthand symbols. As for mathematics, it is often treated as extremely abbreviated language, that is, without much adjectival or adverbial qualification, and while many historians of science think that they can translate everything mathematical into more understandable and less dogmatic "ordinary expression" if given enough time, I am not so sure, since axioms, definitions, rules, and conventions formed by mathematicians can be changed and idealized, and without having clear spatial and temporal meaning or strong value-connotations

Belle: Can't a speaker or writer change the normal value-connotation we associate with a word if it is qualified by a preceding adjective or adverb?

Vera: Yes, and even what comes after a word or both ways as in the expressions "dreadfully intelligent" or "awfully kind-hearted".

Belle: But in most sentences there is qualification?

Vera: Yes, especially as pre-conditioning, intended or expressed, as a way of telling or warning us not to accept a denotative or connotative meaning which follows in a later sentence or paragraph. This can also help trump value-connotation of individual words. In fact, in a sense that is what we are doing now.

Belle: What if one is a philosopher and thinks of denotation as word-reference and not person-determined reference?

Vera: At some point philosophers should learn that most people do not define or use the words "denotation" and "connotation" the same way they do. Nor in terms of actual influence can words refer. People do it.

Belle: Hence the notion that words mean is a non-sequitur?

Vera: Perhaps not formally, but in terms of causal influence, yes. though that idea came to me from Frank. Single words with good or bad connotations *normally* retain them in full sentences, if there is no double-meaning or pre-conditioning.

Belle: Or dead language, secret code, underground mode, shorthand, or mathematics. But you still think that re-definitions change intended denotation, but rarely if ever value-connotation?

Vera: According to Frank, many attempted re-definitions of denotation are often deliberate efforts to re-direct old value-connotations against a new target, and thus become rhetorical tricks to help persuade an audience.

Belle: What about meanings and value-connotations which often change with tone of voice as in irony, fear, love, hatred, humor, analogy, and not just in satire or other feelings and emotions?

Vera: They are the life of every spoken language. Children almost certainly learn more meaning and understanding from a parent's tone of voice than from perhaps anything else. Furthermore, in different moods one's vocabulary tends to change from what is very polite, to "normal", to blunt, colloquial, rude, vulgar, or very loud and violent. We all have different synonyms to fit most different feelings, and if we don't, we at least have different ways of pronouncing them. Let us give examples of what seem like sentences having the same meaning, but in a larger context obviously not. "Please dear, when would you like to leave?" and "Okay, when are you going?" and "God damn it, get the Hell out!"

Belle: Now it is clear why most scientists prefer what sounds neutral and unemotional as if it were objective.

Vera: Yes, we should all train ourselves to seem objective, even if we are "a towering inferno" inside or "unbelievably prejudiced".

Belle" "seem objective"?

Vera: Frank often distinguishes between absolute and relative objectivity, and as if mere objective expression is not enough even to make us relatively objective, if we focus on underlying intent, assumptions, beliefs, or feelings. But strangely, he still prefers objective expression, even if he knows it can be deceptive and misleading. He thinks that being forewarned can protect most of us, without the seducer ceasing to use an objective sounding style to persuade us, even if all human intent, belief, and assumption is actually subjective at least in being mental or psychological.

Belle: He may prefer to seem objective, but I know he can get angry. And when he does . . .

Vera: In fact, he hates rhetoric almost as much as I do, and objectified language is often very persuasive, even without substantial evidence to support the intended meaning or what it is about.

Belle: But where does value-connotation come in?

Vera: Frank worries most about soft-soap persuasion where ordinary words with weak value connotations can appear to be combined with an objective facade, connotations which the victim hardly notices, but unconsciously influences him to lean toward or accept what the seducer wants.

Belle: But why does he tolerate objective façades in that case?

Vera: He warns, warns, and warns readers and listeners to be on their guard, but he still thinks objective appearance is normally better than "honest" emotional expression which can also seduce some people, and from my perspective frighten them into avoiding positions which are criticized.

Belle: Calling ordinary speakers "seducers" seems a little severe. Of course they want to persuade when they talk like everyone does, but that does not mean that they . . .

Vera: Use rhetoric? But if it is value-connotation, weak or strong, conspicuous or inconspicuous, and not evidence which does the persuading, then it is rhetoric and is not right.

Belle: It saves time and we all do it.

Vera: I admit that most expression needs a point and that value connotation can provide it. All Frank and I ask is that people become much more aware if how words without evidence help persuade, so that they reserve judgment more often until relevant weight of evidence is provided.

Belle: You mean help prevent people from being so gullible?

Vera: If more people were taught in school only to believe as strongly as the weight of evidence justifies, that would be a good start, but until then all we can do is present words with bad-connotations often enough to make them aware of how often they are being seduced, yes, seduced into believing what is false or insufficiently supported by evidence.

Belle: I oppose rhetoric, but persuasion is still important, though I agree that weight of evidence should play the most important role.

Vera: I most dislike the use of strongly connoted words which scare readers and listeners into avoiding particular philosophical or other positions. Even justified criticism should not use words with exaggerated value-connotations like farcical, futile, foolish, metaphysical, psychologistic, or meaningless.

Belle: I apologize for expressing the last three terms myself. I shouldn't have let my teachers prejudice me. Bad-connotation can block fairness and deeper levels of understanding.

Vera: Frequently, they have to be prejudiced themselves to effectively prejudice you.

Belle Why?

Vera: Because the feeling that an emotionalist is honest and sincere is normally his strongest weapon, he will often cultivate that impression, and if he believes what he is saying, then the image can even become stronger. Most of us employ bad words when emotional, but it is cold-blooded "surgical application" which frightens me the most, calculated, deliberate, misuse of words and value-connotation, especially about basic classification when employed to help pre-condemn other positions, disciplines, and types of philosophy.

Belle: Can my honor be restored after being so dumb?

Vera: Of course! We can all be conned by con-artists when they find out how we think and what our emotional weaknesses are. But please don't worry about it. Just notice which con-words they use, that is, words with value-connotations, and wait for genuine evidence if the would-be persuader has any to present, before accepting their words, whether emotional, honeyed, "logical", or sophistical.

Belle: But we often don't have enough time for that. We must act quickly on the basis of requests and commands.

Vera: Obeying a request by means of action or even conditional acceptance does not mean one has to actually or fully accept it in mental terms as correct or wise. Nor are obeying all commands obligatory, even in the military, if something unethical or catastrophic is being proposed.

Belle: How many bad words on your list aim to reform the world?

Vera: None, I am not that ambitious. I just want to get the ball started.

Belle: Like Sisyphus?

Vera: Like Roget, his son, and grandson.

Belle: I accepted your idea about shifting from training to education, but if I doubt or question all under-proved claims, then I may lose my friends and alienate a lot of other people in the process who expect me to believe what they say.

Vera: Wisdom often seems anti-social, but if truth matters, then some things may have to be sacrificed, especially blind acceptance of what friends and colleagues tell us, though it is often wise to keep many doubts to ourselves.

Belle: It is natural, especially on technical subjects, to trust authorities in those fields.

 Vera: Neither scientific nor philosophical progress is based on blindly trusting "experts". If we are to improve upon their contributions then at some point we will have to distrust them enough to check on matters ourselves.

Belle: Two points: first, it is not practical to distrust most authorities. And second, in the early days of science maybe we should have doubted a lot, but reliability has increased to such an extent that now it is both foolish and almost crazy.

Vera: I prefer the proverb: "Nothing ventured, nothing gained". Use what authorities say if you like, but don't fully accept anything mentally until you have carefully examined the weight of evidence. Nor does this mean simply reading what *other* people have examined. Authorities should present weight of evidence like everybody else. Nothing is true just because somebody says it is. I admit there are practical problems, but that can never justify gullibility, prejudgment, and jumping to false conclusions.

Belle: Sometimes you are as extreme as Frank. I still can't overcome all of my practical objections.

Vera: Then don't. Experts and authorities have a place.

Belle: But not in philosophy? Right?

Vera: Not in terms of one's best or deepest understanding.

Belle: What about your list of value-connotations?

Vera: I didn't want to list them, but as Frank says, readers and listeners should be warned and forewarned not to use or accept under-supported allegations. They should learn which words and kinds of words scare them most into false belief. I don't know how many I should include yet. It is not easy to form lists of words with good and bad connotations under a system of neutral, denotative classification which can also help readers notice the objectionable terms and their effect in practice while avoiding all use of them ourselves. I will list three types of value-connotation A through C, and each has sub-divisions.

Belle: What do you hope to prove?

Vera: That rare is the sentence with no good or bad connotation.

Belle: To show that language is subjective?

Vera: and mental and capable of seducing people into false belief.

Belle: Even if they do not notice any value-connotation?

Vera: Especially then, according to Frank, because he thinks that a lot of persuasion comes from the little-conscious or unconscious effect of value-connotations

Belle: How about "according to you"?

Vera: As mentioned before, the most noticed value connotations seem most dangerous in my opinion, by scaring people, even you.

Belle: I'm not afraid of "metaphysics".

Vera: Would *you* adopt or retain a position if *everyone else* called it "metaphysics"? That's what I mean.

Belle: I haven't crossed that bridge yet.

Vera: I think you have, when you first accused Frank's position of being "metaphysical". You were simply repeating what your contemporary masters wanted you to say.

Belle: Perhaps I did. But I never crossed the bridge the other way when everybody else accused me. But now I admit that such accusations are unfair in general and now that I understand Frank's position a little better, especially through you, I would no longer criticize him in that manner in particular, though I still think that calling his type of metaphysics "foundation theory" goes too far in the other direction. Its just one semantic position among many others.

Vera: Do you think that language which looks objective really is?

Belle: If after examination there is no value connotation, then yes.

Vera: Even if it is merely a sensory appearance and not really physical?

Belle: I know that you representists think that everything is mental and subjective which is or can be made directly conscious to us, but I find it hard to consistently follow that position in everyday life, even though I admit that visual color and color as light rays are different.

Vera: And are located in different places, the first in our head and the second in external physical objects.

Belle: Okay, language can be subjective in two different ways, first, because of value-connotations, and second, if we accept an indirect epistemology, but I still don't see how meaning as intent can be more objective, except in a relative sense which can always be undone through influence by emotion and prejudice, unless we re consistently careful.

Vera: Support by weight of evidence should make it easier to keep relative objectivity free from emotion and prejudice.

Belle: I can't fight that, but I wonder if what you mean by weight and evidence are really as unambiguous as you appear to think.

Vera: Given the same evidence and the same purpose, I think different people will agree about most things, including weight of evidence.

Belle: Is this an example of what Frank calls "conditional probability"?

Vera: It may be stronger than that.

Belle: You want to persuade me, and I'm working on it, but there is a catch in almost everything, including this.

Vera: Take your time. Rome didn't fall in a day.

Belle: That's not funny. Did you ever try to read Gibbon in less than a month?

Vera: I really meant that logic will survive, even if formal logic does not.

Belle: Because formal language and objectified meaning are not compatible with representist epistemology and treating influence as causes?

Vera: Or with the weight of evidence.

Belle: I will wait until logicians and mathematicians reply, before making up my mind.

Vera: That's a good idea, but you are ready to solve many intellectual problem now. I was very impressed by your discovery that Frank was trying to reverse the old notion that language was more objective than meaning. He had never said that. He often claimed that the objective appearance of language often helped conceal emotional and prejudicial opinions and beliefs, but it was you who pointed out that we can make meaning as human intent and understanding *more* relatively objective and informative than the mere objective appearance of language.

Belle: Was that really me? Did I say that?

Vera: I have to apologize. Frank and I both suffered from age prejudice. Your bad manners and disturbing mannerisms made us think that you were simply immature and half-educated, but you have a real brain.

Belle: Even without going to the Wizard of Oz to get one? You mean I *am* educated?

Vera: More than either one of us thought.

Belle: No, I was lucky. I just pushed the right buttons for a change. Any monkey can do that. Educated? Really? Okay? I'll stop thinking of myself. Lets look at your collection of value connotations.

AI

Bad-Denotative-Connotations

abhorrent, abominable, awful, bad, despicable, ghastly, evil, horrible, terrible, wicked.

Belle: I don't think they are so bad. They don't frighten me. In fact, most people often use them when they try to be facetious or make a joke.

Vera: That's because they are so obvious, but I assure you that if spoken in the solemn tone of voice of a high judge and you are the accused ready to be sentenced that you will remember them.

Belle: Fortunately, scientists and philosophers don't sentence anyone.

Vera: Except to lesser schools and colleges.

A2

Four-Letter "Refutations"

bunk, cant, fake, hoax, junk, mess, scum, sham, trite, vile.

Belle: Few philosophers would dare use such words.

Vera: But there are still a lot of foul-mouthed reviewers, including some waiting to pounce on these very dialogues.

Belle: Who else uses them? I mean besides emotional and angry people?

Vera: Look in the mirror.

196

Belle: Me?

Vera: You wanted to use them against Frank.

Belle: But like a civilized, educated person I refrained.

Vera: Now look at my incisors. Do you want to feel my sharp teeth?

Belle: You're joking. They are not so sharp, rather worn I'd say.

Vera: Everyone who feels insulted, demeaned, or unjustly ignored would like to call your ideas "bunk", "cant", "trite", "vile".

Belle: Stop! You're not serious. I never hurt anybody. Maybe a little dig or touch of satire, here and there.

Vera: Everybody who makes enemies can expect words like: "slut", "trash", "whore".

Belle: Really?

Vera: Every friend surpassed who feels forgotten may hiss: "She's rotten, bad, evil.

Belle: I don't believe it.

Vera: Acquire a position someone else thinks she deserves and words like "devious", "sneaky", and "underhanded" could dribble out.

Belle: Okay, I'll be nicer to people.

Vera: And then they'll say: "What a hypocrite, pretending to be nice when she hates us.

Belle: I never hated anybody, just a practical joke now and then.

Vera: Do you want to hear anymore?

Belle: No, not to my face.

A3

Longer Libels

absurd, asinine, farcical, fatuous, foolish, idiotic, imbecilic, preposterous, ridiculous, silly.

Belle: Why do you call these words "denotative-connotations" instead of "connotations"?

Vera: Because their denotations seem connotative in character. I cannot properly distinguish between them. Like the word "bad", their value-connotation is their denotation.

Belle: But can't one still trace their denotative roots?

Vera: Yes, being absurd was a crime in logic. Asinine suggests an ass or donkey. Farcical comes from farce. I am not sure what the source of fatuous is. Foolish comes from fool. Idiotic from idiot. Imbecilic from imbecile. I don't remember the source of preposterous. Ridiculous comes from ridicule. And silly reminds one of being childish or inconsistent.

Belle: Then they do have at least some denotation apart from connotation.

Vera: Perhaps in the past, yes, but when used as adjectives today all of these denotative sources tend to be forgotten and it is excessively critical value-connotations which rule, so much so, that the connotations have become the effective denotations, just like with the word "bad" itself.

Belle: What I wanted to ask is not why anyone would use horrible words against me, if they had the guts, but why would scholars in the academic world think of doing it against colleagues?

Vera: Normally, they don't. Journals usually prefer neutral words or cleverly weak ones in terms of value-connotation, but are addressed to a special community whose leading members largely know each other and share most interests and basic views, and where disagreements tend to be within narrow parameters and where politeness usually prevails. Let us call this a disciplinary or ideological pale.

Belle: I refuse to belong to any pale.

Vera: Even to any you may be in now? Most fireworks and hence bad terms and connotations are normally directed against unwelcome intruders, ideas widely thought within the pale to be old-fashioned or refuted (which is often mistaken in philosophy), other fields and pales, and especially against all efforts to overturn the basic classification and assumptions on which the pale is grounded or thought to be grounded. A chief defence against revolution in the traditional positivist pale of philosophy of science is to accuse critics and outsiders of employing metaphysical, psychologistic, and meaningless arguments, a defence we have often criticized before as unworthy of any serious philosopher, but many human beings put the survival of their particular pale above honesty and truth, and will probably continue to do so until ethics and willpower become stronger.

Belle: General truths may not apply to all particular cases.

Vera: If properly qualified. The following noun forms also seem to largely disregard source and even literal meaning when employed to mean extreme rejection.

Value-Slander

Balderdash, bombast, bull, claptrap, drivel, humbug, moonshine, nonsense, rubbish, twaddle.

Belle: Here you have added three words to make the needed ten which clearly have denotations different from value-connotations. People commonly use bombast to help refer to exaggerated language, bull to untruth, and nonsense to lack of meaning, though I admit that the word rubbish is rarely employed today by many people to refer as over-criticism directed at literal trash or garbage, even if those last two terms also have strong bad-connotations. I also remember how Plato had trouble accepting certain Forms as real if they had negative or bad-connotations, which seems to suggest that he wanted to keep goodness or at least value-neutrality as an aspect of what he considered real.

Vera: I simply chose ten words for each category for organizational reasons, and it is true that I may not always be able to find "pure" examples to fit that number. I admit that the three examples you have found are "impure" because they do seem to retain denotations from the past, On the other hand, I would insist that the overly-critical, bad-connotation associated with the word "nonsense" is more often used to reject what we disagree with than merely what allegedly lacks meaning, but since the latter use sometimes is intended, even if rarely if ever literally accurate, I have listed the word again with that denotation plus the bad-connotation.

Belle: Even if we support meaning as intent, it is often easier to write as if words had meanings independently of intent and the associations we make with words The better class of readers should not be misled, given how much attention you and Frank have given to meaning as intent.

Vera: Thank you, but I am not sure there is either a better or worse "class" of readers, merely those people more familiar with our underlying volitional position on meaning and those not. We do support free will, at least our version of it, and hence meaning as the particular intent of particular persons at particular places and times.

Belle: Good!

Vera: But in the context of listing words with bad-connotations we have to acknowledge that the connotations we refer to on our list are widespread, though not universal, which can seem to make it more suitable to express ourselves as if words could have meanings independently of both intent and assumptions, even if it is not true either in general or in particular cases. I regret any confusion, but our problem, difficult as it is, is not without solution. It is not a Gordian knot and can be untied. So please do not feel frustrated or resort to trying to cut it as if simplification could avoid over-simplification.

Belle: Your opposition to rhetoric may not fully avoid using it yourself.

Vera: If it is supported by weight of evidence, then it is not always immoral or wrong.

Belle. Even if rhetoric actually does more persuading than the evidence?

Vera: A clever point. But sometimes extensive clarification is more noticeable than rhetoric and can also serve as a kind of evidence. I would like now to turn to listing words which generally have both good and bad-connotations, but where there is a different denotation, one which is not always overlooked.

Belle: How do you plan to list value-connotations as contrasted with bad-denotations?

Vera: By including *both* good and bad connotations. Each numbered section will henceforth start with a topic word like "Age" which will then by divided into two parts such as "young" and "old". We will then list words under "young" with ten good-connotations and then ten bad-connotations such that there will be four lists under the word "Age" and forty strongly-connoted words in all, or the nearest to that number we can find. I cannot do this as well as Roget and his successors, but I will try. His approach starts by contrasting synonyms with antonyms and then listing appropriate words and finally words with good and bad connotations.

Belle: Then why try to amend his thesaurus?

Vera: First, because our primary interest is in value connotations and not in either synonyms or antonyms. Second, he wanted to help people who had ideas and meaning in mind but who couldn't think of the word which exactly fit his intended meaning. And third, He also wanted to *encourage* people to build a larger vocabulary including learning and if need-be using words with strong good and bad connotations, while we want to *discourage* people from using any words likely to mislead others and ourselves, especially in the absence of weight of evidence. He wanted to expand usage and while we largely agree, we want to contract intellectual cheating by helping people become more conscious of the deceptive character of many words while avoiding all words likely to mislead other human beings. Nor does this have anything to do with different levels of language like colloquial, vulgar, and so forth. We are not trying to beautify language which itself can be deceptive given many of our actual beliefs, but make it more reliable where truth is concerned and less dependent on rhetoric and idealized understanding.

Belle: "Cheating" is a strong word, and opposition to idealization can irritate many mathematicians.

Vera: Then soften the first to "illegitimate behavior " and the second to "insufficiently qualified ideas and expression".

B1

In addition to denotative-connotation there is also as already mentioned the approach of *Roget's Thesaurus* based on synonyms and antonyms and which mentions words with good and bad connotations. Below is a passage, page one, from the 1948 (copyright 1922) pocket version.

1. EXISTENCE. – *N.* **existence**, being, entity, subsistence, presence , omnipresence, ubiquity.
    reality, actuality, fact, matter of fact, truth, verity.
    essence, inner reality, vital principle.
    science of existence: ontology.
    V. **exist**, be, subsist, live, breathe; vegetate; happen take place occur, prevail.
    consist in, lie in; be comprised in.
    abide, continue, endure, last, remain.
    Adj. existent, subsistent, extant; afloat, on foot, current, prevalent.
    real, actual, positive, absolute, veritable, true; substantial, essential.
    well-founded, well grounded, authentic.
    Adv. Actually, in fact, in reality, indeed.
2. NONEXISTENCE. – *N.* **nonexistence**, inexistence; non-entity; nullity; nihilism; blank; absence, emptiness, void, vacuum; nothingness.

annihilation, extinction, destruction, abolition, extirpation, nirvana, obliteration.

V. **not exist,** be null and void; cease to exist; pass away, perish, be or become extinct; die out; disappear, vanish. Fade, melt away, dissolve, be no more; die, etc., 360.

Annihilate, nullify, abrogate, tc.,756; destroy, etc. 162; remove, displace, vacate; obliterate, extirpate.

Adj. **inexistent**, nonexistent; negative, blank, null, missing, absent, etc. 187.

unreal, baseless, unsubstantial, shadowy, spectral, visionary. unborn, uncreated, unbegotten, extinct, gone, lost, departed; defunct, etc. (dead)360.

Fabulous, ideal, etc. (imaginary), 515.

Vera: The thesaurus approach not only includes much more than value-connotations and indeed much more than synonyms and antonyms, but many word-analogies as well. At first glance it will seem that bad-connotations far outnumber good-connotations, but that is largely because we are not used to thinking of words like "real" and "exist" as having good-connotations since they seem so ordinary and neutral, but in fact unless modified by prior factors or by qualification they have very strong good-connotations, especially in science and philosophy.

Belle: How is your list different?

Vera: Instead of following synonyms with antonyms, words with good-connotations will be followed directly by words with bad-connotations which represent a kind of severe criticism of the position or positions described with good-connotations above. Also, our topics, while in alphabetical order, will contain two neutral or positive sub-sections and with both good and bad connotations will contain four entries per section. The advantage of our approach should be the brevity and vividness of the value-connotations without the other factors mentioned in a thesaurus. The disadvantages will come from many of the same reasons i.e., lack of inclusiveness.

CI

Age

"Young", plus linked-words with *good*-connotations: *Active, advanced, alert, amazing, eager, energetic, precocious, prodigy, quick-thinking, vigorous.*

"Young", plus linked-words with *bad*-connotations: *bratty, callow, childish, green, immature, infantile, juvenile, milk-faced, puerile, snotty.*

"Old", plus linked-words with *good*-connotations: *Accomplished, erudite, experienced, mature, reliable, time-tested, trustworthy, venerable, well-prepared, wise.*

"Old", plus linked-words with *bad*-connotations. *Aged, antiquated, decayed, decrepit, extinct, fossil, has been, never was, retarded, senile.*

Belle: Have you ever used these words yourself?

Vera: Probably most of them, but in the case of bad words qualified with "not"; nor would I use them to criticize older people. I think that such would be generally unkind and unfair, hence I would like to discourage their use, and help readers become more aware of unjustified abusive terms when employed by anyone, and try to avoid being persuaded by them.

Belle: I don't think most ladies have even heard of many of them. Some men probably have or speakers when they get

Belle: Since many people only want to notice good words and meanings, won't your emphasis on bad ones scare off your audience?

Vera: How can I warn people what words to guard against unless I give examples?

Belle: I'm not sure its wise, but go ahead. What are your next scare-words about?

C2

Belief

"Conditional", plus linked-words with *good*-connotations: *balanced, conditional, fair, measured, moderate, nuanced, open, reasonable, temperate, undogmatic.*

"Conditional", plus linked words with *bad*-connotations: *chicken-out, compromise, cop-out, gutless, half-hearted, spineless, vapid, thin, weak, weasel-out, insufficient (bad-denotation).*

"Unconditional", plus linked-words with *good* connotations: *Affirmative, assured, authoritative, certain, beyond doubt, confident, conviction, positive, trusting, unquestioned.*

"Unconditional", plus linked-words with *bad* connotations: *arrogant, dogmatic, exaggerated, excessive, extreme, naïve, prejudiced, primitive, simplistic, unreasonable.*

Belle: I recognize that people can be misled by the good connotations of words into believing what is not supported by the weight of evidence, but they have a natural appeal which bad connotations rarely have.

Vera: Maybe I should have listed the most famous denotative-connotations of a good or positive kind, and not just the bad ones, but their flattering and hence prejudicial character should be obvious, words like: *grand, great, magnificent, marvelous, splendid, stupendous, superb, terrific, tremendous, wonderful.*

Belle: Many philosophers have acquired followers by praising the abilities and accomplishments of colleagues and students, though William James was probably the most unscrupulous at that kind of flattery.

Vera: I suppose most people like good-sounding rhetoric and persuasion, and even treat it as normal as if without value-connotation, but scientists and philosophers should surely avoid it on the speaking or writing side and try to be cautious and careful when others use it on the listening or reading side.

Belle: But aren't there exceptions?

Vera: Of course! We naturally want to help make people feel better, especially the depressed, unhappy, and less- successful, but scientists should have thicker skins, and . . .

Belle: there ought to be ways to be both honest and nice?

Vera: Yes, but I'm as bad as everyone else, lots of white lies and half truths, just to seem "socially pleasant" and "upbeat".

Belle: That's the current fad, but you can drop out safely, since everyone knows how serious and intellectual you and Frank are. For you both it's just a disguise. You feel you *ought* to be nice and helpful, but your heart's not in it. You believe in free will, and think everyone should always be trying harder to accomplish worthy goals, whether they are happy or unhappy.

You never give up, regardless of how depressed and unhappy you feel, and believe everyone else should do the same.

Vera: You just uttered six "you-words" in the same short paragraph. That's a stylistic no, no. Nor is it clear whether Frank, me, or both of us are meant.

Belle: Stylists beware! I thought only content mattered for savants like *you*. That's number seven.

Vera: I apologize. I have been inconsistent without knowing it. Style can also influence persuasion, and if not backed by strong evidence can be just as bad as other kinds of rhetoric. Please repeat "you" as often as you like. Putting style above content and truth often defines what is superficial. And I did it. Shame on me!

Belle: Thank *you* (that's number eight. Actually, the problem is not logical but psychological. Failure to notice a relation between style and persuasion suggests that you were probably thinking of style as aesthetic and deceptive persuasion as unethical, but if style can contribute to rhetorical persuasion as it often does in the absence of sufficient relevant evidence, then it may be unethical as well, at least sometimes. (number nine)

Vera: As you are probably already beginning to notice, my classification system is beginning to have problems.

Belle: I'm sorry to mention it, but in C3, for example you contrast methods with positions, which sounds fine, but since one can have methods about positions and positions about methods they are not water-tight distinctions.

Vera: Since I should not introduce bad-connotations at either the category or sub-category level but only at sub-sub-category

levels I have not yet found a way to correct the problem as you
can see in the following item:

C3

Classification

"Methods", plus linked-words with *good* connotations:
*appropriate, comprehensive, economical, effective, ethical. fair,
harmonious, orderly, uniform.*

"Methods", plus-linked words with *bad* connotations
*botched, confused, disorganized, incomplete, irregular,
muddled, one-sided, prejudicial, slovenly, unsystematic.*

"Positions", plus linked-words with *good* connotations:
*choose, compare, contrast, evaluate, improve, match, organize,
relate, restore, unite.*

"Positions", plus linked-words with *bad* connotations:
*bifurcate, dismiss, distort, ignore, mangle, mimic, mislabel,
misrepresent, splinter, subordinate.*

Vera: Another type of difficulty arises in C4, namely that
unwittingly the main category "Depth" already has a good-
connotation at least among many scientists and philosophers.
This in turn seems to restrict what can be included as sub-
categories to one of differentiating between matters of degree.
We can still work with it but it is different from how we handle
other categories, sub-categories, and examples, or more
accurately, "samples", since we cannot be inclusive in a single,
reasonably sized dialogue.

Explanatory Causes

"Influence", plus linked-words with *good* connotations: *to arrange, to cause, to change, to do, to ground, to improve, to make happen, to master, to originate, to rearrange.*

"Influence", plus linked-words with *bad* connotations: *cancel, corrupt, damage, destroy, harm, hurt, manipulate, ravage, ruin, suborn*

"Laws", plus linked-words with *good* connotations: *guidelines, legal codes, constants, maxims, patterns, principles, Providence, rules, universals, Ten Commandments.*

"Laws", plus linked-words with *bad*-connotations: *arbitrary, dictatorial, dogmatic, despotic, formalistic, inflexible, non-explanatory, legalistic, restrictive, unjust*

.

Belle: Since you are only giving samples of good and bad connotations and not being inclusive you wisely select many of the more powerful and influential ones, plus a few with scientific or philosophical importance, but your limit of ten samples within each sub-sub-category may be too restrictive.

Vera: Because of the nature of C5, there may actually be more neutral- than good-connotations

Belle: Nor should we overlook that many people treat good-connotations as neutral without noticing any slant.

C6

Fashion

"Simple", plus linked-words with *good* connotations: *cautious, chaste, conservative, demure, modest, natural, presentable, reserved, respectful, unpretentious.*

"Simple", plus linked-words with *bad* connotations: *coarse, dirty, homely, humble, ordinary, plain, ragged, rough, stinks, unpresentable.*

"Sophisticated", plus linked-words with *good* connotations: *accomplished, beautiful, becoming, conversant, discrete, dexterous, intelligent, savoir-faire, tactful, well-dressed.*

"Sophisticated", plus linked words with *bad* connotations: *beautified, clothes-horse, fashion-chaser, exhibitionist, jaded, poseur, snobbish, sophistical, supercilious, theatrical.*

Belle: You show a better choice of words for C6 and there are not so many neutral-appearing expressions.

Vera: I think mastering philosophy is often a matter of understanding more assumptions, definitions, and distinctions which often seem but are not really neutral.

Belle: I liked Greek history, but Frank didn't think I knew enough.

Vera: The deeper one becomes, the harder it is to communicate, and also, to appreciate the work of others. Everyone else seems superficial to him.

Belle: I hope I never become that deep, or superficial.

211

Gender

"Gentlemen", plus linked-words with *good* connotations: *chivalrous, civilized, conscientious, courteous, honorable, just, noble, paragons, trustworthy, upright.*

"Gentlemen", plus linked-words with *bad* connotations: *actors, charlatans, fakes, frauds, imposters, liars, perjurers, mountebanks, opportunists, pretenders, scoundrels.*

"Ladies", plus linked-words with *good* connotations: *distinguished, eminent, elegant, exalted, fair, foremost, gracious, notable, refined, worthy.*

"Ladies", plus linked-words with *bad* connotations: *facile, frivolous, indecisive, insipid, jealous, shallow, silly, vapid, weak, womanish.*

Belle: Please pardon me for being too critical, but I do want to help. Your lists of words with bad-connotations are often more negative responses than either synonyms with bad-connotations or antonyms.

Vera: I agree with that, but it could be connected to one of Roget's discoveries. Since the problem is very complicated to explain, and I am not sure that I can do it accurately at this stage.

Belle: I am not sure what you mean, but could it be connected to John Stuart Mill's attempt at about the same time that Roget published his great work to define denotation in terms of reference, rather than what is normally meant by denotation by most linguists and non-philosophers today?

Vera: I don't know and I am not sure Frank does either. But the question is interesting. Roget's organization of his book suggests he was a direct realist in epistemology and possibly influenced by medical materialism and what was called "Scottish common sense philosophy", but more research will be needed to pin this down.

Belle: Is his introductory system of categories reasonable?

Vera: It is very elaborate and remarkably inclusive without being fully clear in philosophical terms.

Belle: Could you give an example?

Vera: Yes. Instead of talking about mind and matter he subordinates the issue to a distinction between organic and inorganic matter as if he were a materialist, but the other categories he uses cannot be fully subsumed under materialism as normally understood. But in any case he seems to have held a very different philosophical position than Mill. On the other hand, he lists both "connote" and "denote" under the word "indicate" as if made before Mill's distinction between denotation and connotation, but which he almost certainly would have opposed had he become aware of it, since what Mill meant by denotation as if words and not particular persons could literally refer to things makes little sense, that is, for most people who hold that to cause means to influence which is what Roget emphasized in his Thesaurus under the word "cause", and without mentioning "law" or what philosophers label as "constant conjunctions" (Hume) or "necessary conjunctions" (Kant) at all. As a retired medical doctor Roget announced a pro forma materialism and verbally he seems to link idealism with mysticism, but the very unsubordinated inclusiveness of the work and failure to address philosophical issues clearly, means that a lot of reading in his articles, lectures, and correspondence will be required to pin down his actual working assumptions. He apparently wanted to think like so many before and after him that as a scientist he did not have a philosophy, which could mean in practical terms not so much that he was inconsistent about basic philosophical matters as we all are from time to time, but that he may have lacked the foundation criteria necessary even to notice it or to correct it.

Belle: You really are widely educated. I was too ambitious to put myself on your level.

Vera: And I have to admit that you keep surprising me with how much you have already studied and understood.

Belle: I know I still have a long way to go, but I'm tired of the climb. I want to rest for a while, while still being respected for accomplishing something. My motive is ready, but I'm not.

C8

Humor

"to please", plus linked-words with *good*-connotations: *amuse, entertain, be funny, make happy, be humorous, jest, joke, be jolly, be pleasant, be witty.*

"to please", plus linked-words with *bad*-connotations: *abase, beg, bribe, crawl, eat crow, flatter, grovel, stoop, truckle, whine.*

"to laugh", plus linked-words with *good*-connotations *cackle, chirp, chortle, chuckle, giggle, guffaw, Ha! Ha!, roar, scream, titter.*

"to laugh", plus linked-words with *bad*-connotations:
comical, hilarious, laughable, ludicrous, laughingstock, pathetic, make fun of, laugh at, mock, ridicule.

Belle: I don't think that laughing at people is humorous. I think it is cruel.
Vera: what about satire, irony, facetiousness, and laughing at oneself?

Belle: I don't like them, but we cannot always have our own way.

Vera: A facetious tone of voice can change the meaning we give to words, like adding quotation marks in spoken language.

C9

Intent

"to mean", plus linked-words with *good*-connotations:
aim, design, end, goal, plan, point, purpose, deliberate, by design, on purpose.

"to mean", plus linked-words with *bad*-connotations:
bait, blind, bluff, deceive, delude, dupe, fool, gull, lie, mask, spin, trap.

"to be intent", plus linked-words with *good*-connotations
attentive, concentrated, deliberate, determined, focused, prepared, ready, strong, trained, well-equipped.

"to be intent", plus linked-words with *bad*-connotations,
beset by, consumed by, dominated by, haunted by, obsessed by, prepossessed by, prisoner to, slave to, his monomania.

Vera: satire, irony, and humor often rest on double meaning.

Belle: Like: "Never say never"?

Vera: Yes, which is a clever way of warning us about taking a position which we may want to change later. It also makes fun of formal logic.

Belle: Some people are too clever for their own good.

Vera: When in doubt try to focus on the most probable intent of the speaker or writer.

C10

Judge

"weigh". plus linked-words with *good* connotations: *arbitrate, assess, balance, compare, consider, estimate, evaluate, referee, review, take into account.*

"weigh" plus linked-words with *bad* connotations: *biased, bought, hasty, narrow, one-sided, partial, prejudiced, shortsighted, slanted, unfair.*

"decide" plus linked-words with *good*-connotations: *augur well, bid fair, ethical, manage well, moral, promising, rectify, resolve, select, settle, solve, succeed.*

"decide" plus linked-words with bad connotations: *blow, blunder, bungle, botch, dash, fail, flunk, mess up, muff, spoil.*

Belle: You have described three different approaches to value-connotation (A) denotative-connotations. (B) Roget's value-connotations, and (C) your own list of ten samples of value-connotations. But you allegedly have two more approaches. What are they?

Vera: The fourth approach includes three ways to extend (A), (B), and (C). First, while there may be words with bad-connotations like "fail" or "botch" to contrast with words having good-connotations like "succeed" or "manage well" as in the examples above, there can also be bad-connotations seeming to attack other bad-connotations leading into what may seem like the beginning of an infinite regress. For example, some people in criticizing a judicial decision as a "blunder" may be criticized in turn with "overly hasty opposition".

Belle: But aren't you confusing intended criticism with the value connotations we associate with words which seem to stick with the words regardless of our intent?

Vera: Yes, and thank you for the correction. While almost all criticism does involve use of the bad-connotations of words, it is possible to make criticisms with words devoid of value connotation. And if such can be done in practice fine and well. But you are right that I should not have simply taken for granted that all use of bad-connotation implies criticism. A fifth approach, which is actually a way of trying to be relatively objective, is not to avoid value-connotations, but to present both sides of issues such that good and bad value-connotations contrast, and we have partly done that. On the other hand, when a committed party tries to be "fair" it can fail because he is unable to see the other person's perspective from his point of view. One doesn't have to accept it, but one should be able to comprehend it. That is why reading books written from many different angles can help us understand both past and present.

Belle: I know I'm immature and don't deserve your respect as a scholar, but most of my friends still find me more amusing than irritating to have around , and I don't have many friends on your level, largely I suppose, because they are normally more interested in learning and studying than in talking with people my age. But I have a problem. Even with less education I could still help solve some problems as a social activist in my community or even contributing or volunteering to help hungry and starving poor people in Africa, but I am not clear how I could help society more by studying in science or philosophy, becoming a professor, and writing books.

Vera: I would like to be able to answer that you can help a lot more people here and abroad by continuing with your education until you become a teacher or professor, but that is not certain. Still, most of your young colleagues can only help by direct social activity, while you are intelligent and hard-working enough to be able to make a uniquely important contribution to whichever field or fields you decide to concentrate on, and which if you have the ambition and dedication will almost certainly occur, and be much more than you could contribute as a social worker or activist. So it really comes down to how much ambition and dedication you have, and how lucky you will be to find something important that you can discover or improve upon, either from past or current understanding, and how determined you are to correct your own mistakes and also to overcome wrong-headed opposition.

Belle: Thank you for reassuring me about my intellectual capacity. I know I can develop enough ambition and resolve.

Chapter Six

REASONING

Dick: I am a friend of semantics and hear that you have been attacking dictionaries and my field.

Frank: What kind of semantics do you prefer?

Dick: What kind?

Frank: The word "meaning" has many different uses.

Dick: The kind scientists use.

Frank: And what is that?

Dick: That words and propositions mean.

Frank: And what are propositions?

Dick: They are not metaphysical, if that is what you mean.

Frank: Thank you for admitting that people mean.

Dick: That was merely colloquial semantics and not scientific.

Frank: Then you are not always scientific?

Dick: I am actually a philosopher of science, but try to restrict myself to how scientists think.

Frank: Except about meaning and semantics?

Dick: When thinking scientifically, which is most of the time, both language and meaning are objective.

Frank: Even if it is merely a convention and not the truth?

Dick: I also think propositions are objective.

Frank: Even if they are not real?

Dick: You cannot see or touch them if that is . . .

Frank: what I mean?

Dick: Sometimes, pre-scientific habits come out.

Frank; If people associate meaning with words, is it more scientific to say that people mean or that the words mean?

Dick: Since most science is idealized, we commonly say that propositions mean and words mean, but people do *not* mean.

Frank: But particular persons do mean at particular places and times.

Dick: Science aims at laws about types, not particulars.

Frank: And when science is less-idealized and when you want to tell less-idealized or non-idealized truth, and if that is real truth about real particulars, what do you say then?

Dick: That I am not interested in metaphysics.

Frank: Even if the truth is that particular persons mean and not types, propositions, or words?

Dick: Yes.

Frank: So *Argument Number One* is we agree hat people mean in terms of non-idealized science.

Dick: Mathematical chemistry, physics, and astronomy are highly idealized sciences based on the assumption that words and propositions mean, and are almost certainly the most fundamental sciences, therefore, if people mean in terms of non-idealized science, then it is a trivial concession, which is irrelevant or false in the more important fields.

Frank: As a philosopher, which do you consider more helpful? A dictionary or thesaurus?

Dick: It depends. If I need the normal meaning, spelling, or pronunciation of a word, then I will consult a dictionary. But if I want to examine synonyms or antonyms, then I will check a thesaurus.

Frank: Which do you look at more often?

Dick: Like most people, a dictionary, but if I were a novelist or fiction writer, I would probably use a thesaurus more.

Frank: Are history and philosophy fiction?

Dick: Not if one is very careful.

Frank: Can one be very careful in doing non-idealized science?

Dick: Of course. But care about trivia wastes time.

Frank: Can history and philosophy books be written about all fields?

Dick: In principle, but as you have mentioned elsewhere there can even be histories of philosophy and philosophies of history, but since none of either is mathematical or even empirical in a rigorous sense it is all wasted paper as far as mathematical science is concerned.

Frank: Should we burn or junk all paper and electronic histories of mathematics up to the present?

Dick: Of course not. Naturally, survival of past mathematics is important, but mere importance does not make history or even philosophy scientific.

Frank: Unless non-idealized science exists and can be important?

Dick: Okay, I agree.

Frank: Therefore, we agree that *Argument Number Two* about meaning as intent is that as an aspect of non-idealized science it can be important, even for the survival and progress of mathematical science.

Dick: Indirectly, yes.

Frank: Is the intent to be fair objective?

Dick: It can be relatively objective.

Frank: Even if intent is mental?

Dick: If the language used is objective, yes.

Frank: Are words objective?

Dick: In a written language they seem to be, but in a spoken language or where they are merely assumed or intended, I am not so sure.

Frank: Which do you consider more important?

Dick: Written language.

Frank: Which came first?

Dick: Now I see what you are driving at. You want to argue that if spoken language is primary, then there may be a sense in which language is basically subjective. But I rely on generally accepted linguistic conventions and dictionaries which treat language as objective, even if in some obscure or metaphysical way words are subjective.

Frank: Do words have connotations?

Dick: Of course, but you cannot get at me from that angle either. I am only interested in what is objective or can be successfully treated as if it were objective, and that applies to both connotation and denotation, and regardless of how you define them.

Frank: Do people always mean what they say?

Dick: A true scientist does.

Frank: Do scientists ever make assumptions or take anything for granted?

Dick: Naturally. We aim at simple mathematical description, so we have to abbreviate and take some things for granted.

Frank: Are you always aware of what you take for granted.

Dick: Of course not.

Frank: So scientists do not always mean what they say?

Dick: Not entirely.

Frank: Or *only* what they say?

Dick: No. Some propositions are expressed and some are not.

Frank: Do they ever conflict?

Dick: Yes, since we are not always aware of what we intend, assume, or take for granted.

Frank: So meaning may be in the intent and assumptions of scientists.

Dick: Partly.

Frank: Do people associate good or bad connotations with words?

Dick: Yes.

Frank: Is it always fair?

Dick: No.

Frank: Does the word "metaphysics" have a bad connotation for you?

Dick: Yes, but I think it is deserved.

Frank: Does the word "metaphysics" mean theory of reality?

Dick: For some people.

Frank: Is metaphysics incompatible with science?

Dick: Yes.

Frank" Is theory of reality incompatible with science?

Dick: No, but seems to be with much methodology of science.

Frank: How can philosophy of science be legitimate if it rejects theory of reality while science accepts it?

 Dick: Because we are interested in changing science to fit our philosophy.

Frank: You have been more honest and helpful than you think. Do many words have value-connotations?

Dick: Yes.

Frank: Are they objective or subjective?

Dick: While it depends on definition, I agree that value-connotations normally seem subjective.

Frank: Do some value-connotations suggest something positive or good and others negative or bad?

Dick: Yes.

Frank: If words have good connotations are the words objective or subjective?

Dick: Subjective, but most words in mathematical science have no value-connotations.

Frank: Does the word "metaphysical" have a bad-connotation?

Dick: I have answered that before, yes it does, but not for everyone.

Frank: Does the word "science" have a good-connotation?

Dick: The same answer: Yes it does, but not for everyone.

Frank: Does the word "science" have a good connotation for most mathematical scientists and "metaphysics" a bad one?

Dick: Probably.

Frank: If the words "science" and "metaphysics" have value connotations can the words be objective?

Dick: Probably not, but many words in mathematical science are technical and have no value-connotations or at least no strongly negative or bad ones.

Frank: Do words mean?

Dick: No, people associate meaning with words, some with value-connotations and some with merely descriptive connotations.

Frank: Do you accept the notion put forward by many philosophers that words can refer to things.

Dick: No, just as people associate meaning with words as connotation, value, descriptive, or both, so people refer to thongs and it is just a manner of speech to allege that something as passive as words can refer to anything, in so far as reference is understood as a causal process using factual influence.

Frank: Are you now willing to accept as *Argument Number Three* that people mean as both descriptive and value connotation and that words do not mean?

Dick: Yes, and even that propositions as idealized entities like numbers themselves do not literally mean in the sense of intend either, even if propositional talk and reference to numbers is convenient and may often seem essential in much mathematical science.

 Frank: Very good.

Dick: If I may, I would like to take a peek at how your thesaurus is organized, since they group together a lot of words with strong value-connotations, both good and bad, which makes it easier to notice them. But first, who introduced them?

Frank: They seem to have been first introduced by Peter Mark Roget (1779-1869), a medical doctor and philologist who also became Secretary of the Royal Society. From his sixty-first to seventy-third year he combined a very complex organization of his thesaurus with a very simple way of looking up words. But in the process he discovered that in addition to distinguishing between different parts of speech that denotative synonyms were not enough. He also had to add antonyms and also distinguish between the good and bad value-connotations of both synonyms and antonyms, that is, do things which dictionaries should, but rarely do, for space and other reasons. In fact, because dictionaries almost always ignore antonyms and value-connotations they help spread the false opinion that language and meaning are objective.

Dick: And your particular copy of Roget's Thesaurus?

Frank: It was edited by C.O. Sylvster Mawson assisted by Kantharine Aldrich Whiting, and its actual title was *Roget's Pocket Thesaurus*.

Dick: How old is it?

Frank: Please let me first quote from the Introduction by the famous co-author of *The Meaning of Meaning*, I A. Richards:

What Is A Thesaurus?

> "A Thesaurus is the opposite of a dictionary. You turn to it when you have the meaning already but don't yet have the word. It may be on the tip of your tongue, but what it is you don't yet know. It is like the missing piece of a puzzle. You know well enough that the other words you try out won't do. They say too much or too little. They haven't the punch or too much. They are too flat or too showy, too kind or too cruel. But the word which just fits the bill won't come, so you reach for the Thesaurus."

Dick: Please, the year!

Frank: The initial Copyright says 1922, and my edition came out in 1946.

Dick: That was a long time ago. I was tempted to repeat that a thesaurus seems to be more for literary people than for scientists or philosophers, and of course much science and philosophy have developed since then under the impression that language and meaning are objective.

Frank: My paperback copy also mentions that it is the 113th printing from 1922 to 1946.

Dick: Good God! 113 printings is an amazing number, and suggests that your version of *Roget's Thesaurus* was indeed popular, and I would guess so even today, and that more scientists as both students and writers must have often used it. When did you discover that it was important for semantics, science, and perhaps even philosophy?

Frank: I am ashamed to say, only a short time ago.

Dick: I have never heard of a philosopher who even mentioned Roget, much less that he must have assumed that both language and meaning were subjective in his book, or that so many subsequent readers must have assumed that as well. Have you ever heard of a rebuttal or discontent with his approach?

Frank: No, but I am also a "Johnny come lately", to use a colloquial expression.

Dick: You mean about the book's philosophical importance?

Frank: Yes, like most people from perhaps all fields, I have sometimes used a thesaurus, and lately, more than ever, while never thinking about his deeper intent and assumptions.

Dick: Do you forget words so often that you need a thesaurus?

Frank: More than ever. When you push eighty, you should still remember ideas and meaning virtually intact, but very probably, you will have begun to forget some words when you want to recall them, which is why people of my age increasingly turn to *Roget's Thesaurus* or subsequent versions or printings of it, that is, if one is fortunate enough to have one.

Dick: So you look for synonyms in a thesaurus in order to remember words you forget?

Frank: Yes, and such procedure could help almost all older human beings.

Dick: Do you accept the notion that we must learn words in order to expand our understanding.

Frank: Yes, it can help a lot, but about the earliest learning, I am not so sure.

Dick: What do you mean?

Frank: As very young children we often seem to learn much meaning from tone of voice as parents and other children let their voices rise and fall, and gradually we begin to utter sounds which we associate with that inferred meaning, sounds which become words. I do not think words determine meaning, just as neither sounds, words, nor meaning are objective in the learning or remembering process. And this is just as true for scientists and philosophers as it is for everyone else. Particular persons mean in the sense of intend, assume, or understand, which often is or can be made conscious to us by means of the use of language. But such expression is not intrinsic to them, since they can continue to exist without language or expression, though of course there is surely a physical accompaniment in the brain or mind which may not be capable of becoming directly conscious to anyone, but which because of likely causal influence is commonly regarded as physically real or objective

Dick: I have not forgotten some of your earlier points, such as if to be metaphysical means to be real, and one rejects metaphysics, then logically one is rejecting one's own existence, which after Descartes can seem absurd.

Frank: But "metaphysics" has many other associated meanings besides theory of reality, even if that has become the basic denotation, if such a prejudicial term still has a clear denotation.

Dick: I am coming close to agreeing with you, but coming back to Roget's work, since dictionary language seemed to be linguistically and semantically objective to me, but did not include many or any synonyms, antonyms, or what you call "value-connotations", then I accept that dictionaries and thesauruses appear to complement each other, by including what the other lacks, such that if people subjectify meaning the way we do now, then we may regard both as valuable, even if many scientists and philosophers do not. That may be almost as far as I can go to accommodate your point of view.

Frank: Thank you. I appreciate how hard it can be to come even that far. I often think of myself as a mere biographer obsessed with details which most other people ignore as unimportant, but like you, I am happy that I finally discovered the philosophical importance of Roget, even if he was a retired medical doctor and not a philosopher and tried to reduce the distinction between mind and matter simply to one between organic and inorganic matter, but I have a question. What influenced you most, just a minute or two ago, to switch to the opinion that the use of meaning is more subjective than objective?

Dick: Don't crow. It wasn't your logic chopping.

Frank: I'm glad. In fact, I apologize for using it. I don't believe in it and don't like it, and it is not as rigorous as it looks, given ambiguities in meaning and dubious premises. But you came on so hard and fast so I retreated to logic chopping, specially since I didn't have time to emphasize hard evidence, for example, that the purpose and operation of a thesaurus to find the right word to fit our understanding proves that people mean and that words and propositiosn do not.

Dick: Don't blame yourself, I caught the implication even if you failed to draw it, and it helped persuade me.

 Frank: I suppose I must have assumed that since you clearly had a rigor-oriented mind or brain and was already somewhat familiar with my ideas, that you might be just the kind of person influenced by logic-chopping.

Dick: Thank you. I'm glad you respected my intelligence.

Frank: Honest, it was a split-second decision, since you caught me off guard and I fought back with the few resources I had available. I did present the thesaurus evidence with the quotation from Richards, but forgot to pull the string, which fortunately you did for me. I still argue too much, and present evidence too rarely, even when I have lots of it. But if my reasoning was not a major factor, then how in addition to the incomplete thesaurus evidence, what were the other grounds which persuaded you to reject the notion that words and propositions can mean?

Dick" A fair question. I saw that if a primary goal of science is to keep simplifying or idealizing results by mathematical or other methods, then there must be processes of intending, assuming, thinking, and understanding which largely retain a capacity to include, exclude, and modify ideas, also that processes are of a different nature than propositions, and third, that they were probably mental or subjective in some way. And if most mathematical laws and equations are idealized or somewhat counterfactual, then both spoken and written languages as processes are more real and should not be confused with the abstracted spoken or written results of those processes. Nor is scientific language truly objective if it is largely or entirely idealized, especially since it can mean that fictions are more objective than what is real, which does not seem rational. We also violate Occam's razor by accepting a third kind of secular being or existence in addition to mind and matter, "realities" like universals, Platonic Forms, or Popper's "World 3" which some people accept just to be able to claim that propositions, abstract idealities, and other reified fictions truly exist, when in fact processes, mental and physical, are what actually function.

Frank: But earlier you had dismissed such questions as being "metaphysical".

Dick: If a main denotation of metaphysics is theory of reality and if science excludes it, then science becomes entirely idealized or fictional, hence for the sake of science itself, I had to stop criticizing metaphysics and admit that science is concerned with real processes and real human uses of them, regardless of how much we may try to simplify or idealize "types of things" in mathematical science.

Frank: I am normally too argumentative and emotional to help persuade anyone about anything, but I am glad that for the most part you persuaded yourself.

Dick: What a clever rascal you are! And it is my time to apologize . . .

Frank: Opportunistic, I was, clever no.

Dick: for having underestimated your command of logic, especially for "a mere biographer" as you currently call yourself. There are also some interesting implications contrary to Carnap and Popper that some science or at least some reliable understanding of it may also be non-idealized, like history, psychology, and a number of other fields which are not yet as abstract as mathematics and physics.

Frank: Thank you.

Dick: But there are still some "smoke and mirrors" in your approach.

Frank: Really?

Dick: For all your talk against metaphysics because of its bad connotation, you yourself oppose it as theory of reality.

Frank: What?

Dick: You allege that if something secular can be made conscious, then it is mental and subjective, and if it cannot be made conscious, then it is physical and objective, but that is an epistemological distinction and not an ontological or metaphysical one. Both mind and matter could still be made of the same stuff for you, but it is never spelled out, as if you were agnostic about what is real, which is precisely why many positivists reject metaphysics.

Frank: Interesting, but unusual, and possibly far-fetched.

Dick: In identifying what is real with processes, I have at least the beginnings of a theory of reality, but while you talk about things being real all the time, your distinction between real and unreal is unclear, because all you talk about is the distinction between mind and matter which you think are both real.

Frank: I also define reality as what can make a causal difference because it contains energy or can help influence or be influenced by other things.

Dick: That does seem ontological, but says nothing about mind and matter, except to leave open the possibility that mind does not exist or is a mere "epiphenomenon".

Frank: I like to leave possibilities open when I don't know the answer, but unlike positivists I remain interested in possible "metaphysical" solutions. I cannot think of anything more important than inquiring into, studying, and ultimately-discovering what is real. Furthermore in terms of my current understanding, I think that it is much more probable that linguistic processes and meaning as intent and assumptions are mental and hence subjective than that they are physical and objective, though of course I mean absolute and not relative objectivity here, that is, what cannot be directly influenced by what is mental or subjective.

Dick: And if there is no direct influence, then how do mind and matter interact?

Frank: I don't know, but they somehow do as anyone who has felt a conscious toothache from an unconscious physical cause in his mouth knows, like a drill touching an exposed nerve.

Dick: You are still an ontological agnostic, regardless of how "interested" you are in what is real.

Frank: I am a fallibilist. I admit that, but I still think that many things are probably or conditionally real, and I often act *as if* they were fully and definitely real.

Dick: In other words, you are no more certain than your beloved Cicero and Philo.

Frank: Like them, I prefer to be honest.

Dick: I agree about the need to be honest and also that subjectivity as being mental and as being influenced by emotion and prejudice are two different things, but your attempt to subjectify meaning and sensory perception even in a non-prejudicial way may still give opportunities for supporters of religion and mysticism to believe things with insufficient factual or objective support.

Frank: Though I hope that many basic aspects of religion are true, I tend to hesitate if degree of belief would go beyond what the weight of evidence justifies, or if belief is treated as being either total or unconditional belief or none at all, like William James suggested.

Dick: If hesitation is not believing, and some people think any belief is better than none, then many people are likely to reject honesty itself, even if your doctrine of *as if* acceptance and action can handle most practical situations.

Frank: I share your fears, but I think honesty and truth are too important to sacrifice or conceal. Furthermore, it is normally wise to hesitate when understanding and desire conflict.

Dick: May I add a *Fourth Argument on Meaning*, namely, that both the use of language and meaning are processes which seem to be influenced by human intent and assumptions, which in terms of most definitions are regarded as mental.

Frank: I did not suspect that you would add a fourth argument to my three, but since it appears to be sound I will accept it, at least until I think about it more carefully. But my congratulations for your contribution, even if . . .

Dick: I was more influenced by your first three arguments than I realized.

Frank: There are of course more arguments.

Dick: Why do you call them arguments rather than conclusions?

Frank: Because while we argue extensively that meaning is really in the intent and assumptions of particular human beings and that words do not mean and that propositions as idealized fictions do not even literally exist we stand at the beginning of a controversy with the vast majority of mathematical scientists and philosophers plus many other well-intentioned people, such that they will do their best to ignore or refute our perspective, just as you initially attempted to carry out.

Dick: On reflection, much that you said then now seems obvious, but it was so natural to accept dictionary and linguistic habits that words mean and scientific custom that propositions mean that the issue of what is actually true or real simply did not arise, and as you remember I immediately dismissed your point of view as "metaphysical", without really understanding what that was supposed to mean. I just carelessly thought it was philosophical or religious speculation incompatible with science. But if it means theory of reality like ontology or even a restricted version of that, and most scientists not only are very concerned about what is real but often try to discover what exists, then obviously if we can overcome the bad-connotation of the words "metaphysics" and "metaphysical", then we can take a look at ontology as a branch of foundation theory, and try to discover what are some of the underlying assumptions underlying science about what it means to be real, or more accurately different types of science, since many of them seem to rest on different assumptions starting with the differences between idealized and non-idealized science.

Frank: Your mental evolution in semantics could well be repeated a thousand times by subsequent thinkers and scientists, but people change and relapse and when attempts are made to refute what we have called "arguments", then you yourself may well be tempted to return to an earlier position because you may think their arguments are better than ours.

Dick: I will not relapse, and whether our dialogue is either ignored or buried by objections, I will remember our debate and honor you for helping me improve my understanding, though I hope you will credit me for a little originality in thinking of both meaning and language as primarily mental processes.

Frank: In this context, you thought of language and meaning as processes and I did not, and I am happy to credit you with that, though whether they are aspects of or elements in a process rather than the primary or whole process remains an open question.

Dick: As does their relation to physical behavior in the brain as understood in the normal sense of physical, that is, meaning something which contains measurable energy.

Frank: But I am not yet persuaded that because energy does not seem measurable in conscious and hence allegedly mental behavior that what is mental is either non-existent or merely an "epiphenomenon". There is still the possibility that what is mental has some other kind of causal influence than physical energy. It is hard to ignore the possibility that volition and willpower, for example, may have an intrinsically mental type of causal influence.

Dick: You claim to be against rhetoric, but is not persuasion by wishful thinking and logic chopping types of rhetoric?

Frank: Only if unaccompanied by weight of evidence or its easy access.

Dick: So you still don't trust formal logic?

Frank: Not about the real, that is, the non-idealized world, unless properly qualified and supported by weight of evidence. Nor do I approve of working both sides of an argument in order to draw a valid conclusion.

Dick: Sorry.

Frank: At the risk of more wishful thinking, perhaps one day we will see a combination of dictionary and thesaurus ways of treating the relation of meaning to words, relations which also take meaning as intent, meaning as assumption, and both value-connotation as well as measurable tone of voice into account.

BIBLIOGRAPHY

Anscombe, G.E.M., *Intention*, second edition, Cornell University Press: Ithaca, New York, 1963 [1957].

Aristotle, "On Interpretation", *Organon*, translated by E.M. Edgehill, edited by Richard McKeon, in *The Basic Works of Aristotle*, Random House, New York, 1941, pp. 40-61.

Asimov, Isaac, *Asimov's Biographical Encyclopedia of Science an Technology*, revised edition, Doubleday, Garden City, N.Y., 1972, [1964]

Audi, Robert, "Intending", *Journal of Philosophy*, **70** (1973) 387-403.

Black, Max (ed.), *The Importance of Language*, Prentice-Hall Inc., Englewood Cliffs, New Jersey, 1962.

Black, Max, "General Semantics", *Encyclopædia Britannica*, Volume **20**, Encyclopædia Britannica , Inc.,William Benton Publisher, Chicago, London, etc.,1963, p. 313.

Bratman, Michael E, *Intention, Plans, and Practical Reason*, Harvard University Press: Cambridge and London, 1987.

Carnap, Rudolf, *Meaning and Necessity – A Study of Semantic and Modal Logic*, Phoenix Books, The University of Chicago Press: Chicago, 1956. [1947]

Castañeda, Hector-Neri, "Conditional Intentions, Intentional Action, and Aristotle's Practical Syllogisms", *Erkenntnis,* **18** (1982) 239-260.

Chase, Stuart, *The Tyranny of Words*, Harcourt Brace and Company, 1938.

Cicero, Marcus Tullius, *Cicero Selected Works*, translated and edited by Michael Grant, Penguin Classics: Harmondsworth, Middlesex, England, 1965 {1960]

Cicero, Marcus Tullius, *Cicero The Republic The Laws*, translated by Niall Rudd, Oxford University Press: Oxford, 1998.

Davidson, Donald, "Intention and Means-End Reasoning", *The Philosophical Review*, **90** (1981) 252-265.

Davis, Wayne, "A Causal Theory of Intending", *American Philosophical Quarterly*, **21** (1984) 43-54.

Gellner, Ernst, *Words and Things – An Examination of, and an Attack on Linguistic Philosophy*, with a Foreword by Bertrand Russell, Routledge & Kegan Paul: London, Boston, and Henley, 1979. [1959]

Gibbon, Edward, *The History of the Decline and Fall of the Roman Empire*, in seven volumes, edited by J.B. Bury, Methuen & Co., London, reprint edition 1974, originally 1909. [1772-1787]

Grice, Herbert Paul, "Utterers Meaning and Intentions", *Philosophical Review*, **78** (1969) 147-177.

Hayakawa, S.I. (ed.), *The Use and Abuse of Language*, A Premier Book, (Fawcett Publications). 12th copyright, Greenwich, Conn., 1962 [1943]

Hornblower, Simon & Antony Spawforth (eds.), *The Oxford Classical Dictionary*, third edition revised, Oxford University Press: Oxford, 2003 [1949]

Korzybski, Alfred, *Science and Sanity*, Institute of General Semantics: (2nd. Edition, Lancaster, Pa., 1941), 5th edition, 1994. [1933].

Langer, William L., *An Encyclopedia of World History*, newly revised, Houghton Mifflin Company, Boston, 1962 [1940]

Ogden, C.K. & I.A. Richards, *The Meaning of Meaning*, A Harvest Book (Harcourt, Brace & World), New York, 8th edition, 1946 [1923].

Pap, Arthur, *Semantics and Necessary Truth*, Yale University Press: New Haven and London, 1958.

Plato, *The Republic*, translated by Benjamin Jowett, in *The Dialogued of Plato*, Volume One, Random House: New York., 14th Printing, 1957 [1894], 591-879.

Polanyi and Harry Prosch, *Meaning*, University of Chicago Press: Chicago and London, 1975.

Popper, Karl R., *Objective Knowledge - An Evolutionary Approach*, Oxford University Press: London, 1974. [1972]

Robins, R.H., *A Short History of Linguistics*, 3rd edition, Longman, London and New York, 1990. [1967]

Roget, Peter Mark, *Roget's Pocket Thesaurus*, edited by C.O. Sylvester Mawson, Pocket Books (Simon and Schuster): New York, 1946 [1922].

Schiller, F.C.S., *Humanistic Pragmatism* - The Philosophy of F.C.S. Schiller, edited by Reuben Abel, The Free Press: New York and London, 1966.

Searle, John, *Intentionality*, Cambridge University Press: Cambridge, 1983.

Toulman, Stephen, *The Uses of Argument*, Cambridge University Press: Cambridge, 1964.[1958]

Welby, Lady Victoria, *What Is Meaning? Studies in the Development of Significance*, John Benjamins Publishing Company: Amsterdam/Philadelphia, reprinted 1981. [1903]